SURVIVAL AND SANCTUARY

SURVIVAL AND SANCTUARY

TESTIMONIES OF THE HOLOCAUST AND LIFE BEYOND

Translated by
FREDA HODGE

Published by Monash University Publishing
Matheson Library Annexe
40 Exhibition Walk
Monash University
Clayton, Victoria 3800, Australia
publishing.monash.edu

Monash University Publishing: the discussion starts here

© Copyright 2023 Freda Hodge
All rights reserved. Apart from any uses permitted by Australia's *Copyright Act 1968*, no part of this book may be reproduced by any process without prior written permission from the copyright owners. Enquiries should be directed to the publisher.

Reasonable attempts have been made to locate copyright holders, and any potential infringement of copyright is accidental. Should any infringement be suspected, contact Monash University Publishing.

Survival and Sanctuary: Testimonies of the Holocaust and Life Beyond
ISBN: 9781922979155 (print)
ISBN: 9781922979162 (PDF)
ISBN: 9781922979179 (ePub)

Cover image: The *SS Derna* docks in Melbourne, 5 November 1948. Reproduced with permission from Fairfax Photos.
Author photograph: Princess Line
Cover design: Les Thomas
Typesetting: Jo Mullins

 A catalogue record for this book is available from the National Library of Australia

Printed in Australia by Griffin Press

CONTENTS

Acknowledgements vii
Foreword ix
    Paul R. Bartrop
Introduction 1
    Freda Hodge
Translator's note on the testimonies 17

The testimonies

In German captivity together with Poles 25
    Leon Holzer
From Lodz to Bergen-Belsen 33
    Tobcia Blicblau
The Jewish police in Plaszow ghetto 73
    Maria Roza Kamsler
The destruction of Jedwabne 103
    Rivka Fogel
In the camps around Posen 113
    Shlomo Lipman
Once upon a time there was a shtetl, Bendzin 127
    David Tuszynski
The destruction of Zolochiv 137
    Mark Fromer

Addendum: Notes pertaining to the testimonies 143
Notes 157
Bibliography 165
About the author 168

*This book is dedicated to my family,
to help them remember the history of the Jewish people in Australia,
and especially the survivors of the Holocaust
who settled in this country.*

ACKNOWLEDGEMENTS

Without the support and encouragement given to me by a myriad of people this book would never have been written. There are many people who deserve mention, but primarily this book came to fruition due to the cooperation and willingness of the descendants and relatives of the seven survivors, who allowed me to interview them, giving me some insight into the nature of their home life, the struggles which their parents had to overcome, and those which they never overcame. They are Ralph Renard, cousin to Leon Holzer; Sam Kurtz, cousin to Rivka Fogel; Yossi Fromer, son of Mark Fromer; Lorraine Brooks, daughter of Maria Roza Kamsler; Ruth Eckstein, daughter of Shlomo Lipman; Lorraine Schmerling, niece of Tobcia Blicblau; and Elly Brooks, daughter to Maria Roza Kamsler.

I am very grateful to eminent historian and Holocaust scholar Professor Paul Bartrop, who encouraged the creation of this work and who has written the very enlightening Preface.

David Ellinghaus was always willing to go above and beyond in helping me to research something obscure. He always managed to find information which proved to be invaluable to me and never refused to go as far as was possible in finding relatives of the survivors to add to our store of knowledge.

The curator of the Jewish Museum of Australia, Loran McNamara, very kindly allowed me access to the file of survivor Leon Holzer, where I learned a great deal about this remarkable man. The museum acquired the file from Leon Holzer's surviving nephew, Ralph Renard.

The CEO of the Melbourne Holocaust Museum, Jayne Josem, was always encouraging and ready to assist in any way necessary. So too, the librarian, Julia Reichstein, who would respond promptly to any request I had made.

My husband, Norman, willingly read the manuscript many times and made a number of helpful suggestions.

FOREWORD

Paul R. Bartrop, FRHistS

Professor Emeritus of History, Florida Gulf Coast University

In 2018, Freda Hodge published *Tragedy and Triumph: Early Testimonies of Jewish Survivors of World War II*. This was a carefully selected and translated compilation of thirty accounts by survivors of the Holocaust whose testimonies were first published in Munich in the little-known Yiddish journal *Fun Letzten Khurben* (*From the Last Destruction*). Until the appearance of *Tragedy and Triumph*, none of these testimonies had ever before appeared in English. This publication was a singular achievement for Freda Hodge.

With this current work, Freda's rescue efforts have been taken further through the publication of seven additional Yiddish-language Holocaust testimonies, appearing in English for the first time. As with the first volume in 2018, Freda is to be congratulated for her monumental effort in ensuring that these accounts were not lost and are now made available for a much broader readership than would otherwise have been possible had they remained only in Yiddish and seen by a small (and, possibly, diminishing) audience.

Who might be classified as a survivor of the Holocaust is, to a large degree, dependent upon how we define the Holocaust itself.

A general definition could encompass the Holocaust as being the nearly successful attempt by Nazi Germany and its allies during World War II to exterminate the Jews of Europe in a systematic, bureaucratic and state-sponsored campaign. To be a survivor, therefore, would of necessity mean that one was Jewish and lived through this campaign, outlasting the Nazi regime.

For some, however, that is an incomplete definition. The United States Holocaust Memorial Museum (USHMM), for instance, in its website defines Holocaust survivors as 'any persons, Jewish or non-Jewish, who were displaced, persecuted, or discriminated against due to the racial, religious, ethnic, social, and political policies of the Nazis and their collaborators between 1933 and 1945'.[1] On the other hand, Yad Vashem, Israel's World Holocaust Remembrance Center, asserts that Holocaust survivors are 'Jews who lived for any amount of time under Nazi domination, direct or indirect, and survived'.[2]

The difference in definition is important: the USHMM evaluation favours the widest inclusion possible – such that *any* victim of the Nazis is a Holocaust survivor. This demonstrates a certain confusion on the USHMM's part, as elsewhere the website defines the Holocaust explicitly as 'the systematic, bureaucratic, state-sponsored persecution and murder of six million *Jews* by the Nazi regime and its collaborators'[3] (emphasis added).

Yad Vashem, on the other hand, has no difficulty in this regard, focusing its definition exclusively on those who were *Jewish*. That said, Yad Vashem also considers that a Holocaust survivor need not have been targeted directly by the Nazi murder machinery: the definition can include Jews who were not deported by the Nazis, as well as Jews who were forced to leave Germany in the late 1930s.

Yad Vashem also suggests that perhaps the designation Holocaust survivor could include 'all Jews, anywhere in the world, who were still alive by the end of 1945', and 'survived the Nazi genocidal intention'. This wider position is too broad. Yad Vashem itself accepts that 'no historical definition [as to who is a Holocaust survivor] can be completely satisfactory'.[4]

There remain considerable areas of disagreement over who might be described as a Holocaust survivor. For some, it is sufficient to say that any Jew who lived for any period in a country that was ruled by the Nazis, or their allies, is a Holocaust survivor. For others, a Holocaust survivor must be a Jew who was a victim of Nazi persecution who stayed alive beyond the Nazi regime. Many questions remain open: can Jews who lived in Germany before the outbreak of war in September 1939, but left as refugees for other countries, be counted? Is it appropriate to include Jewish victims from Syria and Lebanon (ruled over by collaborationist Vichy France), or Libya (territory of fascist Italy until 1942), or British Mandate Palestine (which experienced Axis air raids during the war)? Is a Jew who lived in hiding, or by passing as a Gentile, or as a partisan in the forest, able to be considered as a Holocaust survivor?

Is it sufficient for a Jewish (or any) person from that period simply to define him- or herself as a Holocaust survivor to be accepted as one? In whose eyes is survivorship defined? Is it an internal or external form of identity? Eight decades after the Holocaust experience, these questions still resonate acutely, and spark debates among researchers, legal experts, politicians, those who themselves were there, and their descendants.

The Holocaust was far from being some sort of grand social experiment into the nature of human existence. Philosophers and theologians will long argue about what the Holocaust signified for the human condition in the long term. Questions as to the nature of revealed truth, the presence or absence of God, and the quality of evil and suffering will be debated *ad infinitum*. For the survivors and their families, however, all these questions and all the words needed to answer them will be meaningless without an understanding of the human dimensions of the Holocaust experience at its broadest, and what it meant to those who lived through it.

Survivor accounts play a vital role in addressing controversies such as this, primarily because the written record – usually compiled by the persecutors – only tells part of the story (and that hardly a flattering one). The very special place of Holocaust survivor accounts means that they need to be treated differently from other sources. These are the reminiscences of European men and women whom circumstances decreed were to be persecuted under inhuman conditions with no guarantee of survival. They came from all walks of life, and from all corners of Europe.

Can such accounts be assessed as reliable historical sources? They deal with events and experiences which the survivors attempt to impart to their readers, often aiming to tell their stories so as to convey the essence of what they went through – though sometimes the clarity is lost in view of the emotional content of the topic being examined. Coming on the scene much later, how are we to assess such material?

While it might elicit factual knowledge, it also (perhaps more importantly) highlights the textures, smells, sights and contours of a person's experience. Survivors thereby tell us what made a special impression on them *at the time*. Thus it is often more valuable than other forms of evidence when trying to recreate the past beyond the dry data of what, when and how.

Survivor testimony should not, however, be taken at face value and without putting it through any tests. Fifty years ago, in an acclaimed debate, Israeli historians Kurt Ball-Kaduri, Zvi Bar-On and Dov Levin undertook to address this issue, particularly regarding the 'best' way to conduct oral history interviews and what one should do with the material thereby obtained. Ball-Kaduri's important essay – 'Evidence of Witnesses, Its Value and Limitations' – concluded that 'it is impossible to set down theoretical rules for such a selective process' as assessing the value of survivor testimony.[5] For example, if a survivor mentions an incident to which he or she says they were witness, the historian can accept or reject their account of the facts based on known context and a broader understanding of the incident being recounted, but they cannot dismiss the survivor's *impressions* of the incident once it is firmly established that the survivor saw it take place. Ball-Kaduri wrote that 'testimony given by five to ten witnesses in regard to the same incident, is valid evidence. But it is not true to say that only one testimony, not supported by other evidence is valueless. Especially in the field of active Jewish life [during the Holocaust] there are cases where only one witness has survived, and nevertheless, or even because of this fact, his evidence is of value.'[6] At the time, this was a highly controversial position, and I suspect there will still be scholars today who will view it with scepticism.

Clearly, every account should be verified where possible, but often it simply is *not* possible. The challenge for the Holocaust scholar is great: given the event-laden historical richness of the period under discussion, it is far from the case that rescuing history is easy. There was an enormous amount of activity taking place in many areas as documented by the perpetrators, but what insight may we gain of such things where no one survived to tell the tale? How does one establish what happened in a community where a population which once numbered several thousand has been totally obliterated? From whom does one obtain eyewitness testimony if all the eyewitnesses have been killed? How does one examine written records where none were kept? Are there any advantages in the historian visiting the site, if – as often happened – it might have been deliberately destroyed by the Nazis? Many hundreds of small villages throughout Eastern Europe were literally expunged from the face of the earth. What happened there? How did the Holocaust manifest itself in these communities? Did the inhabitants resist, or go passively to their deaths? We might never fully know, but the use of testimony, however fragmentary, will start the process of rescuing that history from oblivion.

How do we come to appreciate the fears, miseries and other attributes of life during the Holocaust without recourse to survivor accounts? Where some smaller ghettos were concerned, we simply do not have anything to go on. The same is true of activities in the forests. Again, we are drawn to the conclusion that even one survivor account places us in a better position to understand, and we are thus reliant upon whatever we can find to begin the long process of comprehending the overall ordeal.

Every piece of survivor testimony must be assessed individually, and on its merits. If all that is available are the accounts of survivors – and soon enough, this *will* be all we have left – then we must treat these accounts seriously. In the main, the survivors are attempting to convey what happened to *them*, as *they* remember it. Do they wish to be seen in a particular light? Perhaps. Is their intention to tell the 'truth', as they understand it? Certainly. Do they hope to convey a particular set of images concerning their persecutors, or whether they fought back against them? In many cases, yes. Overall, however, the reflections and reminiscences of survivors are intimate accounts of individual experiences which hopefully they wish to share with others. In many cases, elderly survivors facing their mortality have sought to write down what they experienced before they pass on, and before their stories are lost forever.

The issue of representativeness is also important. In asking how representative an account might be of a given situation, does it tell the full – or only – story? Perhaps not, but it may nonetheless provide insight. As wide a range of testimonial accounts, embracing both the superlative and the inarticulate (and everything in-between), should be employed.

There is no 'right' or 'wrong' way for a survivor to remember their experience. One or two (or even half a dozen) testimonies can never be considered as the last word on the subject without additional corroborating evidence. And as every survivor's experience was intimate to themselves, we must look at it alongside those of as many others as we can find and ask broad questions which might be capable of being narrowed down later. A piece of testimony can no more be dismissed because of its paucity of detail than it can for a lack of sensitivity, or, as psychiatrist Dori Laub has noted in relation to his interviewing of a female survivor, 'my attempt as interviewer and as listener was precisely to respect – not to upset, not to trespass – the subtle balance between what the woman knew and what she did not, or could not, know'.

Quite clearly, neither history nor psychology is the only correct path to understanding. For most survivors, the experiences they describe have become embedded in their souls, and the descriptions they provide almost always recount an atmosphere which is true for them, if not necessarily believable for us. Many provide dates, for example, which we know are incorrect, and in some cases even a full chronological sequence of events is dubious. But we need to bear in mind that those who lived through the Holocaust often operated according to a timescale that was not dictated by a calendar in the same sense that we understand it. Dates that were specific to a person's life, however – the date of their deportation, or on which they left for the forest, or the date of liberation – are usually remembered accurately.

Survivors do not ask us to try to imagine the Holocaust; for the most part, that is not what they are attempting to achieve. For many, it is sufficient simply to tell their story, to record, to bear witness, to show that the world through which they lived was in fact all too real. The challenge is not one of 'imagining' the Holocaust. Rather, it is of conveying to the world an understanding of what the survivor went through, as seen from the perspective of one who was there. They do not attempt to make magic, nor do they attempt to imagine the unimaginable. They simply try to tell the story from their own individual perspective.

Personal testimonies are far from being a 'top up' for other forms of history and can often have as much or more validity than a contemporary government memorandum, a diary entry, a letter or a newspaper account. Their applicability should of course be weighed prior to using them and employed or rejected on that basis rather than according to some more subjective standard – but all accounts have their place. It is just a matter of finding where and how to use them.

The current volume is representative of this specific type of Holocaust literature, in that it is not merely a compilation of previously published material but is, rather, one comprising such material not readily available to researchers, students or the wider reading public. An additional factor is the contemporaneity of its content; these testimonies first appeared within a very short time of the end of the Holocaust in 1945, and, as such, they carry very fresh scars untainted by post-Holocaust reflection or the tricks that age can play on memory.

The value of survivor accounts written in their original Yiddish, as in this volume, is remarkable. For the majority of Holocaust victims and survivors, Yiddish was their primary language. It was how they communicated with each other, and how they communicated their recollections later. In the twenty-first century it is often thought – if thought about at all – that the Holocaust can best be appreciated through the medium of English (or German, French or Polish). But it must be borne in mind that up to 85 per cent of the six million Jews who lost their lives as a result of Nazi actions were people who spoke Yiddish as their everyday language. Extricating survivor accounts from the linguistic confinement of Yiddish is therefore more than just an academic exercise; it is a vital service based on the need to preserve (even protect) the historical record of those who experienced the Holocaust in their very flesh. It is possible to study the Holocaust without recourse to first-person Yiddish survivor accounts, but the pitfalls of doing so are profound.

In this volume, Freda Hodge has assisted us in our efforts to imagine the unimaginable; to obtain a glimpse of a culture that was largely eradicated by the Nazis; to gain new perspectives that might assist us in enhancing our understanding of a phenomenon that all too frequently defies understanding. The accounts here appear nowhere else other than in their original Yiddish, in a largely obscure journal published over seven decades ago. They are worthy of our respect; Freda Hodge's efforts in bringing them to us, our gratitude.

INTRODUCTION

Freda Hodge

When Jewish survivors of the Holocaust arrived in Australia after the end of World War II, they came to a country where Jews had been settled since the eighteenth century. With their arrival, the nature of the Australian Jewish communities would change dramatically. The identity of the early settlers was shaped by the English culture of Australia, whereas the survivors brought with them Yiddish, the lingua franca of East European Jewry, and their distinct European culture. Jewish refugees from other countries naturally introduced several other languages, thus creating a more cosmopolitan cohort in Australia. A new era for Australian Jews began as Jewish culture flourished and Jewish society developed a more confident identity as Jews. Local Jewry had for many years been strongly influenced by the prevailing English culture which had been adopted by the Jewish population, and they initially felt ill-at-ease with the arrival of their European brethren. In order to comprehend this attitude, it is necessary to look at the arrival of the first Jewish settlers in Australia and the subsequent development of a Jewish population.

The history of Jewish settlement in Australia began in 1788 with the European colonisation of New South Wales when the First Fleet brought about 750 convicts from Britain to Sydney. Among them were at least eight, and possibly as many as fourteen, Jews.[1] It has been estimated that of the 145,000 convicts transported between 1788 and 1852, at least 1000 were Jews.[2] Prior to this, convicts from Britain were sent to America, but the successful American Revolution of 1776 meant that a new 'home' had to be found for the unwanted criminal element. Australia was the choice of the British Government as the new destination for their transported convicts. The first penal settlement in Australia was in Sydney, but the difficulty of guarding the convict population adequately in such a large country as Australia saw the colonists turning to the island of Tasmania, where Port Arthur was developed as the new penal colony. One of the prisons, called the Silent Prison, was known as a model prison where a new form of punishment was introduced. Repeat offenders had to remain absolutely silent, forbidden to communicate with anyone for twenty-three hours a day. They suffered greatly from this form of punishment, which was extremely detrimental to their mental health. However, many of the Jewish convicts, their sentences completed, became free men and remained in Tasmania to begin a new life. Others eventually settled in Sydney, so that by 1827 the NSW Jewish population numbered about ninety-five individuals. The later arrival of free Anglo-Jewish settlers on the mainland saw the Jewish community grow and develop into a functioning and well-organised society.

The first synagogue in Australia was established in Sydney in 1844, but in 1864 the building was sold as a result of a split in the Jewish community. In 1878, the community reunited and subsequently built the Great Synagogue of Sydney. The oldest surviving synagogue, however, is located in Hobart, and popular belief about its interesting design is that the architect, having no idea of what a synagogue should look like, designed it in the Egyptian Revival style, popular

INTRODUCTION

in architecture of the time. A second synagogue, in the same style, still stands in Launceston today and continues to be used now and then by the small local Jewish community. Jewish convicts who were allowed to attend Sabbath and Holy Day services in Hobart were required to sit in the gallery where special pews had divisions between them to isolate the prisoners from one another. The Hobart synagogue still functions today, while the Launceston synagogue is opened for worship on particular Jewish Holy Days. The architecture of both synagogues has been preserved according to the original design. The convicts' pews, leg chains still intact, are curiosities that attract many visitors to the synagogue.

One of the most interesting characters among the Tasmanian convicts was Ikey Solomon, a Jew from London. In Dickens' novel *Oliver Twist*, the author modelled the character Fagin upon Isaac Ikey Solomon, a Jewish mobster from London who was a well-known figure in the life of London's underworld. In 1827 the police attempted to arrest him but he evaded capture and fled to New York. The forces of law retaliated by arresting his wife, who was also guilty of criminal activities, and she, together with her four younger children, was transported to Tasmania, then known as Van Diemen's Land. Meanwhile, Ikey was living in New York as a fugitive from justice. However, he was apprehended and was returned to England to stand trial. He was convicted of having carried out eight different criminal offences and was transported to Van Diemen's Land to serve his sentence. He was eventually given his freedom, and from then on he participated in Jewish life and community affairs. Ikey eventually started up a tobacconist business in Hobart. He and his wife had a stormy relationship throughout their marriage, but somehow they remained together. At the age of sixty-six Ikey passed away and received a Jewish burial.[3]

The majority of Jews in Australia retained their faith and began to establish synagogues and Jewish philanthropic organisations, as well as creating Jewish cultural and educational facilities in several towns. Judaism and Jewish culture became embedded in the life of the small but growing community in Sydney. By 1820 the free Jewish migrants who had arrived from Britain numbered a few hundred. As an Anglo-Jewish middle-class group they brought with them many of the practices of English Jewry to their religious life, education and business concerns. Many were professionals and experienced entrepreneurs who were well accepted in Australian society. Jewish congregations were soon established in Melbourne, which was founded in 1835; in Hobart, established in 1804; and in Adelaide, founded in 1836.

Jews participated freely in all the activities of colonial Australia. However, during the late nineteenth century various streams of Jewish immigration to Australia from countries other than Britain saw anti-Semitism manifest itself as the Australian population developed a xenophobic attitude to newcomers and a suspicion that 'foreigners' would change the nature of Australian life.

After Australian Federation took place in 1901, the government formulated a bill to limit immigration into the country, effectively to keep Australia 'white', and to maintain the 'White Australia policy'. There were many obstacles put in the way of would-be migrants from 'unsuitable countries', especially the Eastern European lands. Australian migration officials were given a free hand in deciding who was and who was not a desirable person to become a citizen of Australia. Often this situation precluded Jews from being accepted as suitable migrants.

By the 1930s, Jews from Germany and later Eastern Europe were becoming aware of the dangers facing them as the National Socialist Party in Germany became a force to be reckoned with. Trying to find refuge elsewhere was not simple as many countries were not willing to accept refugees from Europe, especially Jews. In July 1938, the American Government convened the Evian Conference to be held in France. The purpose of the conference was to form an international committee to try to solve the burgeoning problem of Jewish refugees seeking to flee the Nazis and to gain entry into various countries. The Australian delegate to the conference, T.W. White, stated that, at that time, Australia was unable to increase its quota for refugees.[4] Furthermore, he noted, 'As we have no real racial problem, we are not desirous of importing one.'[5] He described Jews as uneducated people who 'invariably engaged in secondhand shop trading and cheap clothing manufacture' and he emphasised that they were 'especially undesirable'.[6]

Before the outbreak of World War II in September 1939, Hitler's successful bid to become Chancellor of Germany in 1933 had given him and his followers the power to establish new laws which impacted the whole German population severely, particularly the Jews. In Germany Jewish civil rights were rapidly eroded, and the promulgation of the Nuremburg Laws on 15 September 1935 made it clear to many Jews that an untenable situation was developing. This gave the impetus for thousands of Jewish families to flee Europe and to attempt to emigrate to countries which they regarded as safe havens. Australia was one such country, and when it had become generally known that the Nazis were implementing their policy of genocide, which was rapidly decimating the Jews in Germany and later in all the territories occupied by Nazi Germany, the Australian Government, despite the prevailing anti-Semitic attitude of many officials, did express its horror at the treatment of the Jews of Europe. However, as Paul Bartrop states: 'When war broke out in 1939, Jews were seen to be a threat to

Australian security as enemy aliens. This observation was exploited as the means to further exclude Jewish refugees, a policy alongside government pronouncements condemning Nazi atrocities during the early 1940s.'[7] This was ironic, and even contradictory, but did not change government policy.

The incongruity of this contradiction was not lost upon those who were becoming more aware of the need to rescue as many Jews as possible.

One of the most remarkable people who believed that it was his moral duty to present a protest to the German Government about the horror of Kristallnacht[8] was Aboriginal Australian William Cooper of the Yorta Yorta tribe, who lived in the state of Victoria. He became a political activist on behalf of his people and the broader Aboriginal population. He led many campaigns for Aboriginal rights against an Australian Government which did not look favourably upon his demands. Upon learning about the violence and bloodshed perpetrated against the Jews in Germany and Austria on 9 November 1938 on Kristallnacht, Cooper brought together a delegation of the Australian Aboriginal League to present a petition to the German Nazi government (at the German Consulate) protesting about their treatment of the Jews in Germany. The German consul did not accept Cooper's petition. Nevertheless, for his courageous stand, Cooper has since been honoured by Australian Jewish communities as well as by the Israeli Government, who have initiated many projects in recognition of Cooper's humane gesture. His story has a special place in the historical section of the Melbourne Jewish Holocaust Museum.

Australia's military participation in the world war may have promoted greater insight among the Australians of the true dimensions of the Holocaust. In addition the press began to give greater coverage to news of the war. The fluctuating attitude of the government towards the acceptance of Jewish refugees from war-torn Europe eventually led to a limited number of humanitarian concessions in this respect.

At the end of the war, when the Jewish survivors were eventually liberated by the Allies, they were temporarily housed in camps in the Allied zones of Germany, Italy and France. Displaced and disoriented, they nevertheless demonstrated the resilience that enabled them to look to the future as they waited to receive entry permits to various countries as far from Europe as possible. Most of the displaced persons were given shelter in the Displaced Persons (DP) camps[9] which were run by humanitarian organisations such as the Joint.[10] Some survivors chose not to live in these camps and were helped by UNRRA (the United Nations Relief and Rehabilitation Administration, a relief agency founded in 1943 and terminated in 1949) and the Joint to find other accommodation. There were approximately 250,000 Jewish Holocaust survivors in the DP camps (later, the number grew, as survivors from Russia began to arrive in the camps), most of whom wanted to leave Europe to start a new life. The majority settled in Israel, but Australia eventually became a haven for about 35,000 Holocaust refugees.

All the refugees had a story to tell after the war, and wanted the world to know the truth about what had taken place during the war years, particularly from a Judeocentric point of view. Each individual's experience during the Holocaust was unique, whether they were in a death camp, in hiding or a member of a partisan group. Historians of the period did not perceive the survivor testimonies to be reliable historical records, and they did not recognise their value. Part of the problem was that many of the testimonies were written in Yiddish and were therefore inaccessible to many historians. Later, however, the historian Michael Marrus addressed the issue, pointedly asking, 'how is the ghastly event of the Holocaust to be recorded by historians? There is no dispute about personal memoirs – valued by all serious students of the subject as a message from a world that most of us scarcely imagine.'[11] After the war, many thousands of testimonies were recorded by various Jewish historical commissions in the DP camps, but, inevitably, many of the She'erit Hapletah[12] did not have the opportunity to tell their stories before they left Europe to seek a new home. Jewish organisations in several of the countries that were accepting Jewish refugees continued after the war to go on recording as many testimonies as possible wherever they were able to do so. Hence, the testimonies that are presented in this work were recorded by a Yiddish Scientific Institute (YIVO)[13] Committee in Melbourne. The She'erit Hapletah were dispersed over many countries in the world, the majority in Palestine/Israel, but also in England, America, South America, South Africa and Australia. America was the choice of many of the survivors who did not intend to emigrate to Israel, and Australia became the country of choice for many of those who wanted to create as great a distance as possible between themselves and Europe. Some survivors had made the attempt to return to Poland and elsewhere in Europe, but many were killed or injured in pogroms carried out by the Polish populace, notably the Kielce massacre in June 1946 when forty-two Jewish survivors were murdered and forty were injured during the pogrom.

Those survivors who were given entry to Australia embarked on a new life that was in stark contrast to the lives they had known in Europe and further afield. The main attraction of their new destination was not only that it was a free country, but it had escaped the devastation wrought by the Germans on occupied Europe. It met the desire of the Holocaust survivors to be as far away as possible from the chaos of Europe, where the bitter memories of pain and suffering and the loss of family and community made it impossible for them to even contemplate remaining there. Given that most of the survivors knew almost nothing about Australia, it was a daunting proposition for them to leave what they had known and to begin again in the unknown. However, most were aware that Jews had been settled in Australia for some time, and this was an encouraging factor in their journey towards a new beginning. The Australian Jewish communities, particularly the Melbourne Jewish population, lobbied the government vigorously to accept their Jewish brethren. In the postwar period when the refugees began to arrive, Australia was a rapidly developing Western country, full of promise and vitality, where the survivors could have the opportunity to heal and to thrive in a democratic society. The restoration of their mental and physical health was of prime importance for the new arrivals, following the pain of their traumatic experiences in concentration and death camps – starving and worked to the point of near death – or who went into hiding. The value of an opportunity to return to a normal life cannot be overstated. However, many of the survivors never fully recovered from their ordeal at the hands of the Nazis. Outwardly, they appeared to be rehabilitated, but in private many did not manage to overcome the effects of their trauma.

Several reasons influenced Australia's change of policy vis-a-vis the acceptance of refugees. For example, the active participation of Australia in World War II, especially after the Japanese had attacked Pearl Harbor in December 1941, and after the fall of Singapore (occupied by the Japanese in 1942), had made them aware that their long-term national safety prospects were rather bleak in the face of growing Japanese military control in South East Asia. They realised that it was necessary to increase the size of the Australian population by lifting some of the restrictions imposed upon would-be migrants. A larger population would be the source of a larger defence force for Australians.

The fluctuating attitude of the government towards the acceptance of Jewish refugees from war-torn Europe eventually led to a limited number of humanitarian concessions in this respect. After the war, a new refugee program was put in place by the now pragmatic Australian authorities. The attitude of the government to new migrants did an about-turn, both to meet the local need for a larger labour force in Australia, and also to meet the humanitarian requirements of the International Refugee Organization's 1947 international agreement.[14] Despite the government's chequered immigration policy, 10,000 Jews (approximately) were successful in entering Australia up to 1945, both pre-war and during the war. From about 1946, there was general recognition that Australia was a fast-developing country that needed additional workers. Refugees and other migrants from many countries in war-torn Europe and Shanghai (where they were given free entry by the Chinese) arrived in large numbers, despite the xenophobic attitude of many Australians; the feeling towards Jews was still inherently anti-Semitic. Popular slang incorporated derogatory terms to refer to Jews and other new migrants; they were often called 'reffos', 'wogs' and 'dagoes'.

In 1946 a large number of Jewish survivors arrived from Europe, but a quota system continued to restrict their numbers. When Arthur Caldwell became Minister of Immigration in 1945, he focused on the need for Australia to increase its population, both for military protection from Asia and also to feed into a skilled workforce to help develop the Australian economy. Australian Jewry had become aware that postwar immigration of survivors of the Holocaust was absolutely necessary to provide for the rehabilitation of Jewish survivors of the war who were languishing in the DP camps of Europe waiting for their fate to be decided. They therefore campaigned actively for the Australian Government to recognise the value of a cohort desperate to re-establish itself, migrants who were willing to work hard, to create new families and to provide a secure future for themselves and their children after the trauma of living through the Holocaust.

Between 1945 and 1954 at least 17,600 Jews arrived in Australia.[15] The general Australian population feared that an influx of Eastern Europeans would be an unacceptable burden and would have a detrimental effect on the Anglo population which had long been settled in Australia. Among the Australian population, there were many who accepted the common stereotypical beliefs about Jews: that they were generally unsavoury and would dominate the country through the banks and the media; that they were unscrupulous and power-hungry and were greedy for money. Cartoons in the contemporary Australian press often featured Jews as caricatures who embodied these characteristics. Anglo-Australians would not have welcomed a government policy that encouraged the arrival of large numbers of Eastern European refugees. Australian Jewry had to argue against the prejudices and suspicions of a population that was still anti-Semitic despite the Holocaust.

The Jewish refugees came with their few possessions to a new land, to a place that offered them hope for a new beginning. They left behind them the carnage of Europe in the aftermath of World War II; they left behind them their former homes, the Jewish lifestyle which had endured for hundreds of years in Eastern Europe and other parts of Europe before being destroyed by Hitler and his regime. Perhaps the hardest of all was parting from their dead families whose final resting places were for the most part unknown.

For many of the refugees Australia was an unknown land, populated by Anglo-Australians and Aboriginal peoples. The Australian Jewish population was English-speaking, although many of them also spoke Yiddish. The newcomers had to learn English in order to fit in with the local population, and they were aware that this was the necessary first step to integrating into a new culture. The refugees headed mainly for Melbourne, where a vibrant Jewish community already existed, and provided a haven for the survivors among fellow Jews. The prevailing Jewish culture helped the refugees to renew their identity, and to find again the dignity of which they had been deprived. Despite the numerous challenges they faced, they were for the most part successful in creating a new home. They brought with them many of the characteristics of 'home'. Among most of the survivors, Yiddish was the mother tongue, and the sound of 'mame loshen' (their mother tongue) immediately gave them a sense of home. A lively social world of clubs, Yiddish theatre, Jewish schools and libraries developed during the next few years. They socialised with one another, sharing their common backgrounds and creating a sense of camaraderie and warmth among their close-knit groups. The survivor community embraced the feeling of family with their fellow survivors, who understood better than anyone else what they had been through. Memorial services became central to their lives. The resilience which had enabled them to survive the horrors of the 'Shoah' (the Hebrew term for the Holocaust)[16] stood them in good stead as they adapted to their new lives. In addition to learning a new language, the new arrivals had to find jobs in order to sustain their families and to provide a roof over their heads, all in an alien culture. Yet they relished the freedom of their lives in their new home. The majority of the survivors managed to succeed financially within a relatively short period, and their children grew up secure in the Jewish culture that encompassed them, as well as the broader Australian culture. However, the memories of the survivors'

INTRODUCTION

experiences during the Holocaust and their tragic losses were never to be forgotten. They haunted some of the survivors throughout their lives.

The testimonies that follow this introduction were given in Yiddish and recorded by a YIVO Committee in Melbourne, which published them in 1949 in a booklet with the title 'Pages of Pain and Suffering'. They bear witness to the bestiality of the Germans in the countries of Europe which they occupied, and they stand as an historical record of the implementation of the 'Final Solution'. They also fulfil the biblical injunction 'Zahor' – the imperative to remember, which appears in the Old Testament. As well as being valuable historical documents, the testimonies are also a memorial to the six million Jews who perished at the hands of the Nazis.

The seven testimonies appearing here are unembellished, and their stark depictions of the victimisation of the Jews under the Nazi regime are highly personalised accounts of the events that overtook them after Hitler came to power; they do not include many details about the survivors' lives before and after the Shoah, but focus on the period of the Holocaust and their time spent in incarceration in concentration or death camps. Their 'aura of authenticity'[17] helps to give the early testimonies their credibility. 'A key concern for all witnesses is the issue of credibility; aware of their own disbelief at encountering the hellish world of the concentration camps, they must have realized how difficult it would be to recount their experiences to the outside world.'[18]

These testimonies were collected very soon after the end of the war, in 1947–48, when the YIVO Committee in Melbourne interviewed six new arrivals in Australia: Leon Holzer, Maria Roza Kamsler, Tobcia Blicblau, Rivka Fogel, Shlomo Lipman and Mark Fromer. David (Devi) Tuszynski, an artist, lived in France, but frequently visited Melbourne, where he had family. YIVO recorded his testimony during one of his periodic visits, when he saw his brothers – one of them, Felix, also an artist – in Melbourne. It was an opportunity for David to sell a number of his art works. One of his drawings hangs in the National Gallery of Victoria.

The primary value of the early testimonies is that the memory of the survivor who is transmitting the data is not yet contaminated by the passage of time and by outside influences such as newspaper reports, radio and film, which bombarded the public. The discussions with fellow survivors of the Holocaust revealed that each one had different experiences in possibly different places. Relatively small numbers of early accounts by Holocaust survivors emerged in the years immediately after the war. The world was not yet ready to hear about the appalling events of the Holocaust. Given these circumstances, Holocaust survivors, who at first eagerly narrated their stories, became reluctant to recount their experiences. The myth about their reluctance to speak about the Holocaust arose out of their disappointment at the lack of interest displayed by much of the world, which seemed to feel that it was better to try to forget the horror and to get on with living. The main emotional outlet for the survivors was sharing their experiences with fellow refugees. It was only in the 1960s, at the time of the Adolf Eichmann trial in Israel,[19] that the public, and eventually historians, began to seriously examine survivor testimonies, and to value them as legitimate historical documents. Unfortunately, the eyewitness testimonies written in Yiddish which were given to the various historical commissions in the DP camps of Germany and elsewhere in Europe were mostly consigned to obscurity for many years. What historians of World War II failed to recognise initially was the value of early Holocaust testimonies for the transmission of history, often revealing minutiae and details which may have been overlooked. As Lawrence Langer has noted, 'Written accounts of victim experience prod the imagination in ways that speech cannot, striving for analogies to initiate the reader into the particularities of their grim world.'[20] In his view they bridge the gulf between history and memory: 'the post-war introduction of the concept "the Holocaust" to describe survivors' experiences, and the adoption of the post-war identity of the survivor as witness, acted as the organizational frameworks for survivors' experiences, enabling personal experiences of suffering to be viewed as essential components of a collective historical event'.[21]

The Jewish survivors who sought sanctuary in Australia found themselves in a country that was not only far from the physical chaos of postwar Europe, but was only on the periphery of the confusing changes taking place in the West, such as the Cold War, the different political alignments of the Americans and British, who now faced a new enemy, one who was formerly an ally but now transformed into the totalitarian communist Soviet Union and its subjugated cohorts. The Americans and the British regarded communism as a great threat. Additionally the American attitude to the Germans, the former enemy of the Allies, was now softening, as the Cold War tightened its grip on the postwar world, creating confusion for all war refugees. In contrast, the 'Down Under' country of Australia offered the peace so necessary to the survivors in their efforts to rebuild their lives.

They deeply appreciated the sanctuary and the physical comforts offered by Australia, but their nightmares haunted them. It was not unusual for some of the survivors to have experienced a permanent change in their personalities. Some were unable to forge loving relationships with their offspring or their spouses, whom they married in order to create a new family to replace those they may have lost, resulting in family dynamics being fraught with difficulties. Although the Holocaust survivors who found sanctuary in Australia were filled with hope that they could build a new life in this country, they carried with them for the rest of their lives the scars and effects of their traumatic experiences in the camps and in hiding from the Nazis. They were never fully free of the ghosts of their terrible suffering under German occupation.

TRANSLATOR'S NOTE ON THE TESTIMONIES

The seven testimonies in this book provide a small window into the vastly different experiences suffered by the victims. They were originally published by the YIVO Committee in Melbourne in 1949 and I translated them from Yiddish.

The YIVO edition was published with the following Foreword, which I have also translated from Yiddish:

> In presenting the first volume of *Material and Documents from the History of Jewish Destruction* to the wider public, the Melbourne Committee of YIVO was of the opinion that it had taken the first important step on Australian soil to collect eye-witness reports from members of She'erit Hapletah who arrived in Melbourne [very shortly after the end of the war].
>
> It was not easily achieved. There were many obstacles to overcome. The greatest of these was clearly of a psychological nature. For each of those who were able to provide the material – those Jews who had miraculously survived – the writing, or the telling, of their story was a terrible ordeal. Nevertheless, one's own normal future is dependent upon the strength to eradicate, as quickly as possible, the nightmare of pain, cruelty and destruction which persisted for years, to forget as quickly

as one is able those hellish days, and not to return to them even in memory.

It is no mean achievement for the Historical Documentation Commission of YIVO to have made these works available to the general public. Thanks to the persistence of the Commission, we can be grateful for the appearance of the first volume. The members of the Commission were truly committed to the testament of our great Professor Shimon Dubnov[1] who, while being taken to his death, told the surrounding Jews: 'Write and record.' If the history of the largest and most destructive Jewish tale of martyrdom will forever exist for future generations because of a huge collection of materials and documents, it is of the first order to thank the survivors who collected, wrote and created diaries while in sight of death.

The reward for YIVO which, even during the Vilna period, managed to attract young devoted collectors of everything that could be useful for Jewish historiography, is certainly not small. Even in the death camps such a collection was projected, which would later be handed over by trustworthy Poles to the Jewish archive of suffering held by YIVO. In the Introduction (an original copy is lodged with the New York YIVO) the authors write: 'Friends, write, characteristically short and sharp. Short as the days which remain, and sharp as the knives which are aimed at our hearts. There must remain a few pages for YIVO, for the Jewish archive of suffering. Those of our survivors, free brothers, will read and perhaps learn something.'

If they had, while in sight of death, an understanding of Jewish history, it is our duty, our especially great duty, to carry out their wishes and last testaments.

TRANSLATOR'S NOTE ON THE TESTIMONIES

Finally, we regard it as our duty to remember the first President of YIVO in Melbourne, the late Rabbi Chaim Rubinstein, whom we must thank for the appearance of this publication, and who made this possible by making sure of the typesetting, the printing and the paper.

The remaining family of the deceased are faithfully carrying out the will of their eminent and meritorious father.

May it set a good example for our society.

YIVO Committee, Melbourne

A note on names

The spelling of place and personal names calls for some difficult decisions. Many of the multinational names in Europe during the war have different spellings for Jews, Lithuanians, Russians, Germans and others. Whenever possible this book uses the Yiddish version of personal and place names.

Roles of men and women in ghettos and camps in German-occupied Europe

In the seven testimonies that follow, three are narrated by women and four by men.

They generally reacted differently to their situations in accordance with their personalities. However, just as their roles in society are mapped out by social expectations, so they behaved and reacted in accordance with their gender. The Nazis' ultimate goal was to murder every Jew; the methods of achieving this were by gassing, overwork, starvation, disease and impossibly harsh living conditions.

In the pre-war world they inhabited, the skills and values acquired by the women in both Eastern and Western Europe were generally developed while they were growing up in Orthodox, traditional homes or progressive, more sophisticated homes where they were allowed greater or lesser freedom to express themselves. Acquiring literacy, becoming multilingual, having greater contact with the opposite sex or acquiring greater domestic skills depended on the class, financial standing and education of the individual household. Often in Orthodox homes where the male head of the house was a full-time student in the 'bet hamidrash' (house of study) the woman became the breadwinner. She may have run a small business in a shop selling food or clothes. Many ran market stalls where they sold a variety of goods. They had to leave the children at home, the older ones having to care for the younger. The pre-war role of the poorer wife was to be a mother and engage in family duties, while her middle-class 'sister' was frequently allowed to acquire an education, to participate more fully in secular activities and generally to have a broader familiarity with non-Jews. Generally women displayed more initiative in making the most of their situation in incarceration.

The men were mostly literate in both religious and liberal homes, the norm being to send them to 'cheder' (a school for the study of Torah from the age of about three or four). As adults, some men worked as peasants, others in business and still others in various professions. Many were in contact with the political and sociocultural world through newspapers and discussions with their fellow men.

But all of this changed with the start of World War II and the creation of ghettos and concentration and death camps by the Nazis. The women were especially vulnerable and were often harassed and raped. Both men and women were physically tortured, but the men usually had the advantage of greater physical strength to withstand punishment.

THE TESTIMONIES

IN GERMAN CAPTIVITY TOGETHER WITH POLES

Leon Holzer

On 30 August 1939 I was mobilised by the Polish army. In keeping with my designated role as an officer for highly important matters in the Korps Kommando,[1] Number 5 (Krakow), I travelled to Gdynia[2] where I dealt with a number of agencies and undertook an [military] expedition; then I returned home to Krakow where I had my family, my wife and son. My daughter was with me in Gdynia and we travelled home together.

Gdynia was permeated by a sense of chaos. First, the families of officers and junior officers among the war refugees were evacuated from there. The number of trains which left Gdynia was very small and the carriages were full of people. The fact that the families of the war refugee officers were evacuated, running in panic, heightened the chaos. The Gdynia government Kommissar made an announcement to the population calling for calm and unity, threatening that whoever would leave the town on his own initiative would in future not be allowed back into Gdynia. The announcement worked. A significant number of Gdynia's shopkeepers and manufacturers did not leave.

After this, as soon as the Germans entered Gdynia, the local people who remained behind had to leave the town with nothing, and to travel tens of kilometres until they were able to stop somewhere.

I arrived in Krakow on 31 August 1939, and on the following day we experienced the first German air raid. War. I reported to the Korps Kommando, but was not given any particular task. I was sent to the officer cadre where there were ten officers who, like me, were waiting for orders and direction. The waiting was in vain. No orders were given. We were forgotten.

I met several Jews in the officers' cadre: Engineer Josef Tauber from Krakow, Engineer Balzam from Skavinjer, possibly Mishlenitz, and someone named Berger from Katowicze.

Finally, on 3 September 1939, an order was given to us to leave Krakow. On that day the evacuation of the military forces and the civilians and their families began. The packed trains went in an easterly direction. Even at this early stage no civilian Jews were allowed on the trains. Many Jews left the town on foot, others left in cars which were later unlawfully expropriated from them on the way. This was carried out by officers who wanted to escape as quickly as possible. They expelled the Jewish drivers from the cars, expropriated the vehicles and drove off. Our military leaders too fled in such a panic that we could not keep up with them.

A few days later I arrived in Przemysl.[3] The town had already been bombed. One of the largest buildings in the town, near the terminal, was completely destroyed. There were many dead. Among the dead were also a few Jewish families. There was terrible chaos in the town. Jewish women ran in panic in various directions of the town, not knowing where to run to or what to take with them. One woman carried a cushion, another a pair of candlesticks. One woman ran up to me with tears in her eyes, and complained to me that the watchman of her house, a Ukrainian, had threatened that, as soon as the Germans arrived in the town, he would murder all the Jews.

IN GERMAN CAPTIVITY TOGETHER WITH POLES

I left together with my officer cadre going further east until we reached Terebovlia south of Tarnapol, where we had to distance ourselves from the defeated military units and deserters who had run to the area, in order to organise a new infantry brigade. However, when we found out that there was nothing with which to arm the new division, that we could not find even one rifle in Terebovlia, we saw for the first time that it was all a tragi-comedy, that it was an unpreventable catastrophe.

We received an order to march in the direction of Snyatyn, close to the Romanian border, because the Russian army had crossed the Polish border and was marching deeper inland. On 18 September 1939 we crossed the Romanian border. We were disarmed and allowed to carry on. That is how it was with all the Polish military. It was worse with civilians, and really bad when they recognised anyone as Jewish. A Jew could get through if he offered a bribe. In Romania they sent all of us south to Dobrudja from where we were sent by train to an internment camp. Passing by the town of Macin,[4] I turned to one of the local Jewish shopkeepers, Samuel Kindler, and asked him to help me to escape from the internment camp. Kindler sent me to Braila where Kindler's brother lived. There I removed my military officer's uniform, put on civilian clothing, and travelled via the Danube to Galati.[5] With Kindler's recommendation I obtained a place to live with an Adolf Zigler. After spending a few days there, I went on further to Bucharest, and there I presented myself to the local Polish Consulate where I received a pass. I decided to go to France where, as I had found out, a new Polish army was supposed to be formed. As a former member of the First Brigade of Polish Legionnaires, honoured with the Order of 'Virtuti Militari', and also as Chairman of the Central Administration of the Jewish Association of Former

Independence Fighters, I regarded it as my duty to go there of my own accord, where the military were, and together with the other soldiers to continue the struggle against the Germans.

Before I was sent to the front I would often visit Paris where the secretary for the Polish Democratic Party, Professor Yeszi Stefan Langrod from Krakow, was involved in political activities. Thanks to him, a commission with the task of organising an action against anti-Semitism in Polish society was formed. Among others who belonged to the party were the former Polish Ambassador in Washington, Titus Philipovitz; the former Deputy of the Polish Parliament, Doctor Prager; and myself.

The Yugoslavian and the Italian Consulates would not give any transit visas to Jews. The Polish Consulate gave me a fictitious testimonial saying that I am a Christian, and on the authority of this document I received the necessary transit visas. I left immediately and on 10 October 1939 arrived in Paris where I presented myself to the Polish military forces. I was sent to a military camp for training. The atmosphere for Jewish soldiers in this camp was terrible. A malevolent attitude to Jews there very often led to many unpleasant events.

I must go back a short period [of time]. While I was in Braila, Romania, the local police prefect suddenly gave an order that all Poles who are in the town must, within a few short hours, go to the other side of Rina. The reason for this order was that several drunken Polish officers were wandering in the main street and attacked every Jewish passer-by.

In France I was attached to the First Infantry Brigade with whom I went to the front and on 21 June 1940 I came to [Sète?]. The Germans captured us and we were taken to a German prisoner-of-war camp.

I was taken into German captivity as a parutshnik [lieutenant] from the French army, together with a group of Polish military men captured in France, and we were treated as such by the Germans. As a rumour spread among us that Jewish prisoners would be shot by the Germans, I said that I was of the Roman Catholic faith. The other Jewish prisoners did the same. But our so-called Polish officer 'colleagues' immediately 'made the effort' to let the Germans know that we are Jews. Because of this, all Jews – Polish and French – had to vacate the barrack. Altogether we were eighty-six Jews. Our camp was in Edelbach-Gefritz, northwest of Vienna. We remained there for four years. The treatment meted out to us was tolerable. With the exception of the Russian army captives, the Germans generally applied the rules of the Geneva Convention concerning prisoners of war.[6]

At the same time, my family were in Warsaw and I was then in regular contact with them. In August 1942, my daughter and her husband, Solomon Zak, escaped from the Warsaw ghetto and went to Zakopane[7] where they lived illegally with false papers. But they were betrayed, and the Germans arrested them and shot them all. My wife and son died during the struggle in the Warsaw ghetto. In August 1944 all the officers of the French army, Jews, communists and Masons – from all the camps – were taken by the Germans to a special camp in Lübek.[8] It was a punitive camp. As soon as we arrived in this camp, the German officers said to us: 'Whoever comes to this camp, does not leave here alive.'

There were 314 French army officers in the Lübek camp, 308 French Jews and six Poles. Among the six Poles there was someone who had converted to Christianity thirty years before, and another, twelve years earlier. But in the view of our Polish 'colleagues' they were still Jews. The ideological influence of Hitlerism had remained among the Polish semi-intelligentsia and was still obvious. I must stress that during the whole period of imprisonment, we were under the control of the Wehrmacht, who treated us no worse than all other prisoners of war even though we were Jewish.

On 2 May 1945 we were liberated by the British army. On returning to Paris I got in touch with the Joint[9] as I had worked for them before the war. At the request of the Warsaw Joint director, Itzchak Guterman, I managed the aid activities for the Jews in Gdynia. Now the Parisian Joint suggested that I go to Germany to manage the aid activities among the Displaced Persons. At that time the Joint was still unable to send their people from America because the communications link with Europe was not yet established. Our group consisted of five people: Y. Rak from America; Dr Henrik Haylon and his wife; and M. Lambert and myself. On 2 August 1945 we arrived in the DP camp Feldafing, Bavaria. The people in the camp were bitterly disappointed when we arrived, because except for a small pack of mezuzas[10] and a little bit of medicine, we had not brought anything else for them. We were assigned to present a questionnaire for survivors in the DP camps Feldafing, Landsberg and Deggendorf.

The questionnaire concerned survivor hopes of getting visas granting them entry into the countries to which they would like to emigrate. Approximately 20 per cent of the camp inhabitants declared their desire to migrate to Palestine.

More about Leon Holzer

Leon had five siblings: his sisters Iza, Rachel (who became a famous actress in Australia), Heloise and Dosia, and a brother, Henry. The family was well educated and maintained a traditional Jewish home. Leon was reputed to be a mischievous child, and his cousin Ralph Renard, who lives in Melbourne, described how Leon as a child would spit in someone's soup during a meal, knowing that his victim would refuse to eat it, and then Leon would offer to do so, thus getting a second helping. Leon matured into a thoughtful, bookish man, very intelligent, and always following intellectual pursuits. Politically, Leon was both a socialist and a nationalist, fiercely loyal to his former country, Poland.

Leon and his second wife chose Australia as their preferred destination and arrived in Australia in 1947.

In the National Archives of Australia[11] there is information concerning Leon Holzer, a new immigrant; his personal details are listed for government records. He was born in Krakow, Poland, on 23 April 1895. At the end of World War II, after liberation, he and his wife served with a Joint unit and UNRRA (the United Nations Relief and Rehabilitation Administration) in the American Zone for two years. He travelled to Australia on the ship *Ville D'Amiens* and arrived in Sydney on 19 July 1947, as a stateless refugee, with his wife, Irma, born in Bielitz, Poland, who was a biochemist by profession. He was met by family and travelled with them by train to Melbourne. Very soon after settling there he was employed by Richard Pratt in the Pratt family's new company, Visy, established in Melbourne in 1948. Leon and Richard were acquainted with each other from Danzig, where Leon had been able to help Richard obtain papers that enabled him to leave Poland. A close friendship developed between them and lasted for Leon's lifetime. His employment by Pratt's Visy company was a symbol of the loyalty between them.

There was more to Leon than was generally known. *The Hebrew Standard of Australasia*[12] published an article about Leon Holzer in July 1947 and introduced it with the following words: 'Among the Jewish migrants who have come to Australia in recent years [there] have been not a few who fought for what was then their country.'

These words applied to Leon Holzer, who stood out among these newcomers as a heroic soldier in the Polish Legion from 1914 to 1921. He received several awards for his bravery, which included the Virtuti Militari, the highest Polish award for valour, and other decorations. Another publication, *The Daily Telegraph*,[13] published a short article accompanied by a photograph of Leon wearing his old Polish army uniform. In the article he is described as a holder of the Polish VC (Victoria Cross). The title of the article is 'Polish V.C. Immigrant'. At the start of World War II, when the Germans invaded Poland in 1939, Leon escaped to Romania, to Italy and then to France. In France he was commissioned by the army and served on the Maginot Line. Together with his unit, he was later captured by the Nazis after their invasion of France. He was sent to a German prisoner of war camp where he was incarcerated for four years. There, the Jewish prisoners attempted to pass as Christians, but anti-Semitic Polish officers revealed that they were Jews.

Leon's liberation was followed by a two-year period spent in Landsberg DP camp. When he arrived in Australia, he was questioned by the Australian authorities about his service in the Polish army. Mention was made of the many awards given to him by the Polish army, but he stated ironically, 'I do not propose to go to Warsaw to get them. Instead, with my wife I have come to Australia to find peace.'[14]

FROM LODZ TO BERGEN-BELSEN

Tobcia Blicblau

On 1 May 1940 the Lodz ghetto[1] was completed. During the early days food was obtained opportunistically. For a while food parcels were received by post from the provinces. Food was also smuggled in from the Aryan side outside the ghetto. Later all this was stopped and bitter hunger ensued. The question of heating was even worse. Little by little wood stolen from the Marysin[2] district gave some relief. At one time Marysin was inhabited by Christians but it was now part of the ghetto. We stole trees and fences; we tore pieces from houses and in this way we heated our homes.

At first the only sources of income were from various types of work for those serving as 'officials' of the Judenrat [a Jewish administrative council established by the Nazis ostensibly to represent the Jews and carry out German orders] under the management of Rumkowski, as well as numerous types of private work for the Germans: shoemaking, tailoring, maintaining the ghetto and also harvesting vegetables, potatoes and other foodstuffs which were grown for the ghetto. Those who worked in maintenance were called 'white-guards' because they lived especially well, and earned well from all kinds of sources.

At the end of 1940 the situation deteriorated. The inflow of food was almost completely at an end. At that time the Germans stated that people could voluntarily register for work in Germany. A large number of men actually registered and were sent to Germany. My brother Shlomo, whose whereabouts I do not know until the present day, was among them.

For those who remained in the ghetto, 'resorts' – or workshops – were established for the German war effort. They manufactured shoes, clothes and women's military outfits. There were also laundries for washing clothes, among which were clothes brought from the front, military clothes which were covered in blood. Socks too were made, as well as gloves and ear-muffs. There was also a straw workshop. Shoes for the soldiers were woven from the straw so that during the coldest months their feet should not freeze. [These were worn over their regulation boots.] A metal factory was one of the largest of their undertakings. There they manufactured machine and car parts. Everyone in the ghetto had to work. The Germans even destroyed the schools, and children from the age of seven were sent to work.

In 1941 they started deporting people from the ghetto. The main victims were the children, elderly people, and those who were unfit for any sort of work. Already by the beginning of 1942 many of those people born in Lodz were 'missing'. However, the Germans brought in Jews from other cities around Lodz. In the summer time, about June, they brought in Jews from the provinces: Zgierz, Ozorkow, Brzeziny, Dvart, Sieradz, Kalisz, Lask, Torek, Pietrkov and generally from all the surrounding areas. Jews from other countries were also brought in – from Vienna, Austria and Czechoslovakia.

A few days after those people were brought in, the Germans carried out a raid which lasted for eight days. During this time everyone in the ghetto had to be in their houses and not venture out into the streets. No food was available during this period. At the time of the raid the Germans attacked whole blocks of houses, and the residents were taken into the courtyards where selections were carried out: the elderly, mothers with their children, and young people who looked poorly were removed from the rows and transported in trucks. At the same time all the hospital patients were liquidated – both the seriously and less seriously sick, and those who had recovered and should have been out of hospital. They were taken away and transported. At the time it did not occur to anyone that people were being taken to their death. In Lodz people knew about work camps, but not about death camps.

The selections were carried out by the Germans with the 'death's head' on their caps. They were helped by the Jewish police, among whom there were different types of people – good and bad. I myself clashed with a Jewish policeman who would not let me pass so that I could save my life during a selection, even though he could have done it without any danger to himself. He pushed me with his foot. But I saved myself while I was on the way in a wagon which was driven by another Jewish policeman. He said to me: 'If you are able to save yourself, then do it.' I jumped down from the wagon and ran. After the raid, 'normal' life was resumed.

In 1941 we had the mildest winter. We still had a few possessions, something to burn in order to warm the houses. We simply smashed up our own furniture which we then used for heating. Later we didn't have even that. We slept on the floor, hungry and very cold.

The most difficult year was 1942, the most bitter year in every respect. Later we did not feel as needy, because those who could endure – mostly physically robust people – became accustomed to everything. In 1942 in the streets one saw many people swollen from hunger. People collapsed in the streets, fell dead at their work in the factories. At home it was terrible. Ice covered not only the windows but seemed to grow on the walls too. The bedclothes were wet and cold. Whole families died from hunger and cold, they simply lay down to sleep and no longer woke up. The number of dead every day was so large that no more funerals were held. The dead were collected and placed on large wagons and they were taken away to be buried. The mortality rate among the Viennese and Czechoslovakian Jews was enormous. They were suddenly thrown into hell before they could become accustomed to the hardship as we had, the majority unable to withstand the suffering.

Life in the ghetto continued as normal, so to speak. Between one selection and another we worked and lived even when the most necessary items in the house were confiscated. Nevertheless, we could not take our own lives. There were people in the ghetto who lived very well, lived in abundance and warmth. This was Rumkowski's clique. One might say that they lived in luxury. In Marysin, Rumkowski organised a sort of harem of young girls. There they got drunk and behaved wildly all night. Rumkowski, already an old man, got married in the ghetto to a young girl. In addition to this, he still had the harem in Marysin where he would often enjoy himself together with his closest workers. The 'white guard' members,[3] who stole from the 'provisions camps' and sold the goods on the black market, also lived well. Those who worked in the co-operatives lived very well too.[4]

In about 1943 a secret youth organisation whose young members were from different political parties – Bundists, communists, Poalei-Zion and Hashomer – was established. The organisation stated that its main task was to sabotage the work carried out in factories. The main concern of the factory managers was to get more work done.

For this reason Rumkowski gave bonuses: extra gifts of food for greater productivity. Most importantly, the foremen put pressure on the people at work. In every factory there were young people from the organisation. The best-run factories were those where metal work and tailoring were done. I too belonged to the youth organisation. We encouraged each other to work as little as possible. But we learned how to carry out our actions. The Germans started watching us, and if a foreman noticed anyone he regarded as suspicious, for example, a person who spoke too much to his fellow workers, that person was put on the black list, and during a selection those on the black list were among the first to be summoned for transportation.

In the ghetto there were Jews who collaborated with the Germans, spying on other Jews in the ghetto and passing on to the Germans all sorts of information. It was enough if someone was seen to have a ring, or a fur coat or some other item; then that person would be denounced. As long as these people brought items to the Germans, they were allowed to live and some were even rewarded for their work: they were given extra food rations. When this ended they were transported and liquidated.

Despite all the suffering in the ghetto there was a Yiddish theatre which was of a high standard. Variety shows were presented: new ghetto songs, ghetto humour and satire. The theatre existed until shortly before the liquidation. The shows appeared once every two or three weeks. The theatre was always full. About 500 people could fit into the hall. Tickets were not expensive. People saved from their meagre earnings and attended the theatre. The ghetto had its own currency, metal and paper. Printed on the money were the words 'Litzmannstadt-ghetto'. On the paper money there was also a picture of Rumkowski with his signature. On the opposite side of the note there was a Star of David.

Ever since the arrival of the Germans in Lodz until the lockdown of the ghetto, Jews had to wear yellow armbands on the left side. After the lockdown of the ghetto until its liquidation, we had to wear them on our chests and on our shoulders on the left side, sewn on yellow patches in the shape of a Star of David. They were approximately ten centimetres in size with a black printed word on it: 'Jude'.

The liquidation of the Lodz ghetto began in August 1944. The chief official in the ghetto was Biebow: as it was said, 'Goering's brother-in-law'.[5] During the beginning of August 1944, Biebow called all the Jews in the ghetto to assemble in a large square where he gave a speech, something to this effect: 'Because the Russian front is getting closer, and because the Jews worked for the Germans, it is certain that when the Russians arrive in Lodz they will kill all the Jews. Because until now we have taken care of you,' Biebow said, 'we want to take all of you out of Lodz, and to take you with us to Germany'. Biebow assured us that we could take with us all the possessions that we wished to, and that nothing would be plundered in Germany, where we would work and be together with our families.

But people no longer believed all these good promises. No one volunteered willingly. Biebow gave such speeches to the Jews several times, calling on them specifically to go to the assembly points in order to leave. No one volunteered. Therefore an order was issued that those who were summoned and failed to appear would be shot and their families punished. On this occasion a certain number of people did comply. They began to be afraid. Those who did not come forward no longer appeared at work, and hid themselves in cellars and other places. My brother Mendel was among those who did come forward. His decision to go with the others came about because he did not wish to put our whole family in danger. Those who went were actually allowed to take with them whatever they wanted. They took factory tables and tools for work. Because the group of volunteers was quite small, Biebow ordered that the others be taken by force. Soldiers surrounded whole streets, searched the houses, and took whomever they found and sent them away.

I, my sister, my older brother, my parents and a few other people, my father's friend and his wife, were hidden in a cellar. Each one had with him a bag of food. When an attack on our area took place everyone descended to the cellar. When things settled down we returned to the house. We survived in this way for a week. On 16 October our quarter was attacked. We sat in the cellar and heard the commotion outside: the crying of children, the shrieks from the adults, and, above all, the shouting of the Germans. When our whole courtyard was completely empty and the Germans had begun to move away, we suddenly heard the voice of a policeman calling out that down below in the cellar there must still be someone. A German ordered him to go down to see who had disappeared into the cellar. Immediately the policeman, with an electric lamp in his hand, descended into the cellar. We recognised him. He was the Jewish policeman, Shemiatitzki, who lived together with us as a neighbour in the same courtyard, at Zsgerzsher Street, number 15. We asked him not to betray us, and to say that he had not seen anyone there. But he replied that he was unwilling to risk his life for us and demanded that we get out of the cellar.

We all went out into the courtyard. We were then taken to the railway line and were loaded on to a large freight train with tens of wagons. Each of us was given a loaf of bread, a quarter of a kilo of sugar, and a little bit of soup before we entered the wagon, which was quickly closed and locked from the outside. The train started to move just before nightfall. No one knew where the train was taking us.

The next day, at about noon, the train stopped. From the small window of the wagon we could see only blocks of houses enclosed by barbed wire. We saw no people outside.

The train remained stationary like this for two hours. The sight of the barracks and the barbed wire affected my father badly.[6] He experienced a premonition that something bad was going to happen. We, the children, comforted him, saying that all would be well as it had been until now. At about two in the afternoon there was a sudden commotion, a stir, Germans speaking, and the opening of the doors of the wagons began. When the wagons were opened we saw in front of us many armed Germans in khaki uniforms with black ties and armbands on which were swastikas, and others in black uniforms with the death's head on their caps. Then we saw people wearing striped clothes: white and blue or grey and blue. They were prisoners, camp inmates. We heard ominous calls: 'Out of the wagons, take nothing with you, men to the right, women to the left.' Whoever did not follow the orders on the spot received blows. They beat them on the head with sticks. We heard crying and screaming from men, women and children, mingled with the wild shouting of the Germans. Families wept as they began to part from one another. We too parted from our father and brother and told our brother to keep watch over our father. Our father repeated that we should watch over our mother. Shortly afterwards we were separated. Each one of us believed that only the men and women were separated, that the men would remain together and the women would remain together. They began to chase us women forward, and the men were left behind us. After only a short distance, we arrived at a place where some Germans were standing, and they began to separate the old from the young and the children. Thus my sister Roza and I were separated from our mother.

I wanted to go with my mother, but I was pushed back again. When I looked around I no longer saw her. She had already disappeared somewhere.

I and my sister were arranged in lines together with all the other young women, and under the watch of SS women we moved on. In the lines the cries and the moans were terrible. The SS women 'comforted' us, saying that we need not get upset because every Sunday we would get together with our parents who were taken somewhere else. We continued to walk for a long time. On the way we met Russian prisoners of war who were working at digging trenches. We were terrified by the appearance of those people. They were broken down, skeletal and filthy. They appeared half-dead, not human. Crying out, they asked us to give them something to eat. We threw pieces of bread to them, and this made them fall upon the bread like wild dogs. We continued further until we were led to a large building.

Inside the large building was a great hall divided by a barrier where on one side there stood women who looked healthy and who were well dressed. Later we found out that they were kapos.[7] We stood on the opposite side – hundreds of women crammed together. Suddenly a door opened from which some men emerged, some in military dress and others in civilian clothes. We were told to undress. Fearfully we looked at each other; around us there were men so we did not want to get undressed. We asked who these men were, and we were told that they were doctors. Willingly or unwillingly we had to undress. Naked, with only our shoes in our hands, one at a time we began to cross the barrier to where the women kapos were waiting. These women stopped every one of us and took away from us whatever jewellery we had on ourselves: rings, earrings, watches. After that we entered a long corridor flanked on either side by rows of men. These men looked at every passing woman, and if someone was not so attractive or did not look too good, or perhaps had a defect, or even the least little spot on her body – that person would be led into another room. We never again saw those who were led into the other chamber. Together with the others we were taken into a large room where we stood naked for several hours. Suddenly, a number of women wearing white overalls entered with shaving equipment in their hands. The women did not say one word to us when they started to shave the hair from our heads and other parts of our bodies. After everyone was shaved, we were led to a bathroom with shower heads, where women were packed together as tightly as possible. The pressure was terrible; it was impossible to move. Then they opened the taps and we were drenched with water. After keeping us in the showers for a long time, they then led us, wet through, out of the baths. At the exit, women in white aprons washed the heads of each one of us with carbolic soap. Again we entered the large room where they kept us locked in for a long time. We stood there as if we were in another world, stunned, each one unable to recognise the others. I called my sister who was standing near me and she didn't reply – she did not know me. Then women kapos entered and distributed dresses among us. They were filthy, blackened rags, soaked in disinfectant and they stank awfully. They deliberately wanted to humiliate us when they distributed the clothing. They specially chose to give a tall woman a very short dress, a short person received a very long dress. Each garment had writing on the back with a cross in front of it. Not one of us looked around to see what sort of dress we had received, only that we could cover our naked bodies. When we had dressed we were driven out onto the street. We were assembled in rows and guarded by women kapos; then we were taken away. We walked continuously for about two hours past barracks, blocks and gates. Finally we stopped at one of the gates, and several SS men counted us, registered our names and led us into the camp.

We were taken into a barrack: at the entrance, on the left side, a corner was set aside where the block elder lived. Further on there was a shelf on which stood a row of very large pots. A very long oven was built along the full length of the barrack. Along the walls there were bunks of four levels on which we slept. Those who did not have a bunk to sleep on found their place of rest on the bare earth. For that reason they were given covers – one cover for four women – while those who lay on the planks received no covers.

On the first night none of us slept. We wept over our dark fate. Here for the first time we really felt our loneliness. The wailing from the bunks and from the floor was awful. With all the wailing in the middle of the night, the block elder came in with her assistant, the 'housekeeper', with clubs in their hands, and insisted that we calm down. They not only spoke, they also beat us mercilessly, and that night more than one of us was beaten until the blood flowed. At about three in the morning we were awakened by the loud call: 'Get up!' We were quickly chased out into the courtyard. It was dark and cold. We were given a few minutes for our natural functions and for washing ourselves. Along the length of the barrack there were four devices with taps – that is where we washed. The shoving at the taps was indescribable. We had to use our elbows. Whoever was stronger accessed the taps. On the other side of the barrack there was the toilet: a long row of hacked out holes in concrete. Here too it was very difficult to find a vacant place. Barely having emptied our bowels and washed a little – and many did not manage to do so – we heard a whistle, the signal for the 'Appel' (rollcall). We were arranged in rows of five and we stood like this in the cold until nine-thirty in the morning. If by chance someone became tired of standing and sat down for a while, everyone was punished by having to kneel while holding rocks in our hands. At ten o'clock an SS man and an SS woman arrived to conduct the Appel.

At those times when new transports were brought in we were all locked up in the barracks so that the camp looked empty. We found out from those people in the camp who had arrived before us where we actually were, and what is done there to the people. We were informed that we were in Auschwitz and that here people are cremated. In this way we finally lost all hope of eventually seeing our parents. Gradually we became accustomed to the thought that today or tomorrow all of us could be taken away to be cremated. From the old inhabitants we were advised not to get too close to the wire around the camp because it was electrified. More than once during nighttime we actually heard the ghastly screams of a woman who, in despair, threw herself onto the electrified fence in order finally to find her death.

At about twelve during the day there was a new signal for the Appel. This time the Appel was not conducted by the SS but by the block elders – themselves prisoners, women of different origins – even Jewish women. That was the midday Appel. A large container of soup was brought for our row. We were divided into groups of five and each group had a pot from which only that row drank the apportioned soup from the container. There were groups of five who were reliable and decent, who behaved well towards each other while sipping the soup. There were others who fought with one another. The stronger ones grabbed most of the food and left almost nothing for the weaker ones, nor did they allow them to even come near the pot. Like animals those groups fought over every drop of soup.

The food consisted of a very sparse and thin soup made of potatoes or peas. Frequently soup was made from the food looted from the newly arrived transports. Every new arrival would bring some food – bread, potatoes or flour – but all of this was expropriated, put into the pot and cooked. This time there was such an awful mixture of soup with different flavours and smells – a mixture without taste. But people fought over every bit of food and the stronger ones always had more and better. The block elder who stood near the vessel and distributed the food helped stir up the provocation, the bitterness and the violence among the hungry crowd. A line of people generally stood in front of the large vessel, and the block elder would suddenly move the pot to the opposite end of the line, so that whoever had previously been the first in line suddenly became the last. This would cause pushing and shoving. The block elder would use this simply to be malicious. First she would call on the people to calm down, to restore order; but try talking to a hungry mob. If it did not help, the crowd would again start pushing, hitting and yelling, and the block elder would take the whole container of food and pour all of it onto the ground.

What did hungry people do at such a time? They hurled themselves onto the ground and licked the spilled soup like animals.

In the evenings we were chased to the bunks very early and then locked in the barrack. Then the nightlife of the barrack began.

The large, long oven was heated, not in order to warm us, but to be used to cook a meal for the block elder and her assistants from the barrack attendants. Together they consisted of five people. They had enough bread because all that was meant for us was not really distributed to us. A large amount of it was taken by the block elder for herself and her people.

They also found a way to acquire food to cook. The block elders had access to many places in the camp, and they were friendly with the kitchen workers, and also those in the food stores, in the camp offices, and the garment workers in the factory. A considerable black market functioned among all these people, bartering goods for other goods, food for other food, whatever someone needed. In this way the block elders had whatever kind of food in whatever quantity they needed, and in the evenings in every barrack they cooked special meals for themselves and the barrack-service people. It is understood that the cooking was a secret kept from the Germans. Often the oven had to be switched off in the middle of cooking, and water was poured over it if they learned that the SS was conducting an inspection.

Bit by bit we learned to live with our sorrows, we became accustomed to our new situation, and at night we slept quietly. Thus several days and nights passed. For the time being we were not sent out to do any sort of work.

On the tenth day, during the Appel, both my sister and myself became part of a group of 250 women who were separated from the rest. The group comprised only young and healthy-looking women. We were removed from the camp.

We walked for several hours until we arrived at another camp. There we met many people from Lodz, including two young women whom we knew – the two Schlesinger sisters. In Lodz we had lived in the same building. The younger one, Basia Schlesinger, is still alive; the older one, Sara, died in the camp.

We were registered once again, taken to a small house from which a man and two women emerged, dressed in white aprons. Again, a medical examination took place. Again we were told to undress completely, and each one of us had to march past the man and the two women. The young and well-built were allowed to pass, the older ones and poorly built or very young girls were detained. I was asked whether or not I was pregnant. I answered that I was not. Then she asked me if I had lived with a man. When I answered 'no', she said to me: 'here, if you want to, you will have the opportunity to live with men.'

From our group of 250 women, twelve were stopped and not allowed to pass. The remainder were taken to a large field. Around us there were barracks. In the evening, groups of people who had worked somewhere all day entered the barracks. We found out from these people that the camp in which we found ourselves was called Birkenau. In this particular camp we did not come across many Jews. The majority were Christian women – Polish, Ukrainian and Czechoslovakian women who had had numbers tattooed on them towards the end of 1941.

We stood in the field until late at night. In the distance we saw a whole row of places from which flames could be seen. We asked what the flames were about. One of the guards, a Christian, himself a prisoner, answered us: 'Do you not smell it?' And truly we smelled a peculiar stench around us, a bitter and asphyxiating smell. And the Christian added: 'They are burning gassed people in the crematoria.' We did not believe this. No one was able to believe; it was impossible to believe such a horrifying thing.

At about midnight we were lined up in rows and taken to the baths. Before the baths we were ordered to undress completely. It was raining hard and we stood like this under the open skies. We stood naked in the downpour for long hours until they allowed us to enter the baths. After the baths they distributed new clothes: trousers, a shirt, a striped dress and a pair of shoes. When we exited from the baths it was already dawn and we were on the opposite side of the camp. We did not see the fires again. We were then taken to the railway line.

They loaded us into cattle wagons and gave us food for three days: a piece of bread with a piece of wurst [sausage] and we were on our way. We travelled for three days. During this time, the train stopped several times along the way, and each time a few wagons at the end of the train were uncoupled. We then carried on with the journey. We were locked in during this time, without a drop of water. In order to carry out bodily functions we had with us a bucket which quickly filled up, and this accompanied us for the whole journey. The stench in the wagon was horrible. A number of people became ill while we travelled. On the third night the train came to a standstill and we were let out of the wagons. We went on foot and passed through a small town which was dark and dismal, until we arrived at a place with a large gate through which we passed. We found ourselves in an area between two blocks. We stood all night in this place. In the morning we found out where we were, that this was Ravensbruck.

We remained in this area for twenty-four hours. On the second night we were led to the baths. After we had showered ourselves, we were again given new clothes and we were taken into our designated block. It was a block which housed gypsy women.[8] For two weeks we lived in that block together with the gypsy women and we did not have even one restful moment, neither during the day, nor by night. The block elder and the service personnel were gypsy women who hounded us to do various types of work which they themselves had had to do before we arrived. They also took from us the bread ration which had been apportioned for our use. At night we were unable to sleep, we did not undress because the gypsy women stole everything they could from under our hands.

After two weeks we were again made to bathe, given our underwear, and we returned the dresses in which we had arrived, and then we were sent away.

After travelling by train for three days, our train stopped and the wagons were opened. Polish women worked alongside the railway line and from them we found out that we were in Leipzig. The whole station had been destroyed by bomb strikes and the Polish women worked at clearing up the ruins.

For a whole day we remained at the station guarded by the SS. At night the wagons were locked and the train moved on. Again we travelled for three days, but this time without any food at all. On the third day the train stopped, the wagons were opened and we were told to alight. A number of the military arrived together with German civilians. One of the military men presented himself as the chief of the camp and said that he was now taking over us and we would be under his command. While departing from the station we saw a sign: Mülhausen-Thüringen.

We walked through the Mülhausen streets. It was still quite early. In the streets people were going to work. They looked at us as if we were wild creatures. We must have really looked wild: shaved, in concentration camp uniforms, afraid, filthy and exhausted. I think that we did not resemble humans at all. Having covered a small distance, we came to a line of streetcars which were waiting for us. After half an hour of travelling on these streetcars we came to the back of the town. After a short march, we arrived at a place which was surrounded by barbed wire. That was our camp.

We were taken into a large canteen filled with tables, decorated with Nazi flags and draped with pictures of the Nazi Führer. We were ordered to sit at the tables and we were served coffee, a bed cover was given to each one of us, and they allowed us to sleep overnight in the canteen.

In the morning we were given black coffee and bread, and we were led into the courtyard. Hay was distributed to us for filling the sacks on which we were to sleep, and in addition each person received another two bed covers so that each one had three blankets. Each person was also given a bowl, a pot, a spoon and a knife, and we were told that all these objects, all of these possessions, belonged to us. This decent treatment made us feel rejuvenated, feel human again.

The following day we were divided into groups and sent out to work. Before we left for work, the Kommandant of the labour camp told us what we would be doing, that we would be given light work – we would make small watches. These were really watches, that is to say, watches of a special kind. They were 'watches' [timers] for V2 rockets.

Our factory was in a forest a few kilometres from the camp. In the camp there were large factory buildings which were camouflaged against air raids. Spread out on the roofs of the buildings was earth in which trees and grass had been planted. High walls surrounded the buildings so that from outside it was impossible to see what was happening inside.

In the factories we had no contact with the SS nor with the military, only with German civilians with whom we even became friendly after a short time. Their behaviour towards us was very good: some of them even helped us secretly, in whatever way they could – clandestinely giving us a piece of bread or other food, because we did not get much to eat there either. I took up all of my time working on one screw, a small screw. I worked on thousands of these little screws.

The system in the factory was bearable. The Appels were carried out quickly without any additional harassment. The counting was done rapidly and we were not tormented. Work started at seven in the morning; at ten o'clock we had a ten-minute break; lunchtime was from one until one thirty – good thick potato soup with grain or noodles. Work finished at six o'clock. During the day the work was often interrupted because of air raid sirens. As soon as the alarm sounded we would go down into underground bunkers. Generally speaking, in this sense, the factory was well organised. The canteens and the bunkers had electric lighting, water, toilets and chairs for sitting down. It is understood that all these things were not done for our benefit. Before we arrived there Germans carried out the work and all these conveniences had been arranged for them. We took their place in the factory after they were sent to the front. The factory and the surrounding forest were often bombed but not one bomb hit the building. The Allied aircraft searched for the factory but were unable to detect its actual whereabouts.

I worked in the factory for seven months, from approximately September 1944 to March 1945. During the last few months the factory often stopped work because of a shortage of electric power. The increase in bombing made things more difficult. We would sit for days in the factory, waiting until work again commenced.

There was a hospital in the camp, serviced by a doctor from Buchenwald, which was the central point for our camp. In both the camp and the factory we did not know each other's names, only our numbers. Each one of us wore on our clothing a sewn-on number on the left arm and a yellow and red Star of David with the letter F on it. Only the number was used to call anyone.

For the whole period that we were in the camp there was only one fatality among about 250 women: a young girl died from a brain infection. The sanitary conditions were good. Every fortnight we were given clean underwear and a bath. Sundays were free. There were Appels where we were counted and afterwards we were left free to do as we wished in the camp.

We had no information about the present situation (for the military or for civilians), how the war was progressing, or that the Germans were suffering from one attack after another. Next to our camp there was a camp where Russian women were interned. They had more freedom of movement than we did. They could even go into the town. One day one of the Russian women threw a letter over to our side. The letter stated that we should persevere, that the end of the war was approaching, that 'our people are almost here'. This was the only information which we received about the situation.

On 1 March 1945 the work in our factory suddenly stopped. Actually, a few days earlier one of the German overseers had secretly told us that we would probably be sent away from there because the front was coming closer. We did not believe it. Yet, when the work stopped we saw that something was really happening. In the camp there was a commotion. We had to return everything that we had received when we arrived: the bed covers and the dishes, and then at night we all left together with the SS men and women and the Camp Kommandant. The camp was destroyed.

After a few days of travelling we arrived at Bergen-Belsen. We were taken into a block with no windows or doors. We spent a terrible night in that block. Five hundred people were packed in like herrings in a barrel. We lay one on top of another. It was impossible to move even a limb. The stench was appalling. In the block there were toilets, trenches without sanitation channels. In a matter of a few hours the trenches were full, the raw sewage overflowed onto the ground where people were lying.

On the following day a number of people from our group were sent to work in the kitchens and storerooms, and a second group to which I belonged was sent to a place where there were a large number of people who had not been used for labour. People were sent here to die, unable to survive disease, hunger and cold.

Bergen-Belsen was divided into two parts: one part where people who were used for different types of work were held; and a second section where people were incarcerated in a state of filth, hunger and cold. They were mostly sick people who had been in labour camps. When they had become ill they were sent there to die. The daily death toll was incredible. Here no food at all was given, the quarters were filthy, lice and bug ridden. People here were eaten alive by vermin. Those who dragged themselves around were no longer human nor ghosts, but the living dead. We were sent there, although our group belonged with those fit for work. Whether this was by chance or not, who can know? We were in that section of the camp for a few days. On the third day, suddenly a group of Germans entered; they saw that there were a few healthy people wandering around and they removed us from there and sent us to work.

We worked in the storerooms where old clothes were kept. We cut long strips from rubber coats and tarpaulins and afterwards we made them into 'plaits', making knots which were needed for military purposes, for explosive materials. Also, there it was incredibly filthy; lice crawled all over one's body. In our spare time we did nothing but delouse ourselves. We removed our clothes and cleaned the lice from them.

We worked from dawn until late at night. We weren't aware of time, as it were. We worked like automatons. At night we were brought back to the barrack, exhausted and worn out. We got onto the bunks – each a narrow plank for four women. We hardly washed. In our block there was a large wash room which was locked in the morning and opened only at night. But very few women dared to go to the wash room to wash a little of the dirt off. They avoided the wash room because they were afraid of being beaten there. The block elder, a Jewish woman from Czechoslovakia, took a special pleasure in entering the wash room, and, without a reason, would beat the half-naked women over their heads and bodies with a stick. So we were covered in dirt and almost never went into the wash room.

A neighbouring block which was for men was encircled by barbed wire. The men in the block had been there for quite a long time, and every morning during the Appel we saw in the open field, where the Appel took place, tens of bodies which had been collected, and thrown on top of each other. The death rate among the men was generally higher than among us women. Every morning during the Appel, while counting the people, the Germans would determine who was missing: dead, sick or escaped. Escaping from there was almost impossible; therefore, every night, from every block, even the dead had to be carried to the Appel. After counting the living, they counted the dead, and established whether they matched the general number or not. Thereafter everything was in order. The Appel was concluded without any incidents.

Not far from our block there was a place which was surrounded by a high fence. It was impossible to see over the high fence what took place there. We could see only a protruding high chimney which at times belched out corrosive smoke. There was a crematorium there; that is where they burned the dead bodies. There were no gas chambers in Bergen-Belsen, but there were enough people dying daily without gas chambers, so the crematorium had sufficient work. Every day there would pass by our gate on their way to the crematorium wagons fully loaded with corpses to burn. On our way to our workplace we saw, just in one spot, huge stacks – mountains of shoes, all sorts of shoes: men's shoes, women's shoes and little children's shoes. They [the Germans] removed everything that the dead had on them and took them naked to be burned.

For three weeks we worked in the place where we made the 'plaits'.[9] Suddenly they moved us to another place where we undertook different work. In one of the large barracks there was a storeroom for military clothing: uniforms, trousers, socks and various other items which a soldier requires, such as needles and thread and a variety of other things. We had to transfer the goods from that huge storeroom to another place. Many of us took a chance and stole various things in order to be able to barter them for different goods, mainly food. There was considerable trade going on in the camp, bartering one thing for another. It was like that in all the camps. I also risked stealing a pair of socks. It appears that someone informed the Germans that there were thefts going on, so suddenly, after work, we were all taken to an empty barrack where we were required to voluntarily give up all stolen goods that we had with us. If we did not do so, we would be beaten. Immediately after this the search began. It is understandable that each one quickly threw down onto the floor everything which we had on us. There were some who were caught and they received terrible blows from sticks and fists, so much so that not one of them was left without broken bones. There were those who received blows beneath their lungs and heart and shortly afterwards died from the beating.

When we had finished working in the storeroom, they sent us to work in a forest. We had to chop down trees and afterwards to drag them away. The SS men drove us cruelly, hounded us to drag the trees more quickly. The trees had to be pulled as far as the crematorium gate. There men were working and they dragged the trees further into the yard. The gate was open so that I was able to see what was happening inside.

I saw trenches which had been dug and in them were laid layers of wood and then layers of dead bodies to be burned. Some graves were already filled and the layers of wood and bodies reached several metres above the ground. Our work group was called 'wood-kommando'. In addition to the strenuous labour and the constant urging us on with our work, supervising us, we had an SS man who used to come to the forest with five dogs. As if it weren't enough having the devilish SS men pushing for us to work harder, they would set the dogs on us, and a number of us would return from work every day bitten and wounded by the dogs.

At that time many new transports arrived in Bergen-Belsen. New people arrived in their thousands, perhaps tens of thousands. The camp became so full that in the barracks there was a shortage of space for each individual. There were so many people that they did not know what to do with them. The lack of space and the crowded conditions made the control in the camp slacken. People took advantage of this. I and my sister decided that we would no longer go to work in the forest and that we would hide ourselves.

In four days' time, in the morning right after the Appel, we left our line and mixed in with the crowd. We had to keep hidden for the first few hours until the wood-kommando would go off to work in the forest. We hid ourselves in various different places: in a toilet, in a trench, in a corner somewhere, changing the hiding place all the time until a few hours had passed. When our group had already gone, we returned to our barrack. There we contacted the block elder who was unable to give any advice to people like us because there were so many of us. She swore, she shouted, she threatened to expose us to the Germans. By this time it was all the same to us whatever she did. We were exhausted, devoid of any strength, so depleted that each one then decided on his or her own: whatever will be, will be. The block elder attacked us and beat us fiercely, but this didn't help either. Those who had decided that they would no longer go to work in the Katorz forest would not weaken. It ended in the following way: the block elder replaced the workers from the wood-kommando with other people, and sent us to do different work, digging trenches.

At a fenced-in area we had to dig trenches according to a set measurement for the length, width and depth: 150 square metres per trench, one and a half metres deep. On more than one occasion my sister and I did not attend work. The following morning, after Appel, we would leave our row and steal away. On one occasion we hid for several hours in one of the kitchen blocks. By chance there I met three girls whom I knew and with whom I had worked in a bayonet factory in the Lodz ghetto. They were the three sisters: Loibe, Regina (I don't remember the third one) Gliklich. It is thanks to them that we were able to hide for a few hours until we were able to return to our block. The block elder greeted us with lots of shouting and cursing and declared that she would send us to another block, that she no longer wanted to keep us there. She wanted only those who were willing to work, and the following day she really did send us to another block where my sister and I remained for approximately four weeks and worked at various types of labour. We were no longer able to hide ourselves. We were chased to work with sticks, all of us without exception – the sick, the swollen, the half-dead. But there, in that block, we lived to see the hour of liberation.

Liberation came on 15 April 1945. During the time that we were in that block we no longer received any bread. We fed ourselves on rotten turnips cooked in water; an epidemic of typhus broke out in the barrack among those lying on the floor and in the bunks. Weakened by a high temperature, the sick, half-dead people, eaten by lice, and burning up from their temperature, were unable to move from their place and soiled themselves. At the time there was complete chaos in the camp. The toilets, just like the barracks, were no longer cleaned. Discipline was so undermined that the block elders were no longer able to control the people who were under their command. The number of sick increased from day to day, from hour to hour, while at the same time the number of dead rose daily. You might be speaking to someone and a few minutes later the person was no longer alive. Gone. We lay among the dead, we ate and we slept among them. We made an effort to drag the corpses outside behind the door, and mountains of the dead accumulated there. Suddenly the water in the camp stopped running. Only one working pump served the whole camp. But it was guarded by the Germans and they let no one near it except for the kitchen workers. Sick people with high temperatures dragged themselves to the pump to get a little water with which to moisten their dry lips. But these sick ones were brutally beaten. In the camp there were several walled reservoirs that were filled with water in case of a fire. The water was dirty and stinking but people used this water. On one side people washed their dirty clothes, and on the other side people stood and drew water to drink.

I too was sick, emaciated – skin and bone. I had a fever and on my body there were blue marks. I lay on the bunk weary and without any will. My sister lay near me. Three women lay on one bunk. This was already spacious because previously there were four or even five lying on one bunk and those that didn't have a bunk had to lie on the bare floor. One could say that now there was enough space on the bunk; in any case, more than before. With the passing of time there were many people who died, and since no more new people came, there was more room for the survivors.

I didn't know that liberation was really close. No one knew. Until almost the day before liberation the Appel was still taking place. We made an effort to drag the sick out; the severely ill were taken out to the Appel place and seated on benches. In the last few days before liberation the block elder's demeanour to us was a little nicer. It was evident that she knew something or guessed what the situation was. Therefore she allowed the very ill to sit during the Appel, but nothing good came out of it for those people. During the Appel those people who were unable to stand on their own feet, whoever was sitting on the bench, was sent to a special barrack where the seriously ill were left without any care; they were left lying until they expired. Very few of these people were able to endure for long enough to remain alive and to experience liberation. For that reason, during the Appel people made the effort to stand on their own feet in order to avoid being sent to that barrack which was akin to a death sentence.

One day before liberation no more Appels were called. No one in the camp knew anything. The thought that the end might have come did not occur to anyone. People were happy for the fact that they left us alone, we were not dragged to the Appel, and we were left to lie undisturbed.

The following day, the day of liberation, from very early in the morning there were no more Germans to be seen in the camp. Hungarians, armed and wearing white armbands, wandered around the camp. The fact that we no longer saw any Germans in the camp already aroused everyone's curiosity. It was soon understood that something had happened. The news that there were no longer any Germans in the camp spread rapidly among everyone. But it did not make any special impression on anyone. Complete apathy existed. At about two o'clock in the afternoon, they [the Hungarians] came into the block and announced that tanks, English tanks, were entering the camp. This immediately evoked a strong reaction. Sick people close to death used all their strength to drag themselves out of the barracks into the courtyard in order to see with their own eyes the English tanks, to see liberation.

Weeping broke out among all the camp inmates, weeping from happiness. However, there were many who did not understand at all what had happened and did not respond at all, because they were so dulled and weakened.

I barely managed to drag myself out into the courtyard. My sister remained lying in the bunk. I saw the English tanks. They were loaded with people. English soldiers stood on the tanks and waved to us. I did not know what was happening to me. I returned to the barrack to tell my sister what was going on outside, that I personally had seen the English tanks, English soldiers, and I spoke to myself and asked: is it really true that we are free, is it not a dream? I could hardly believe it.

Later the English tanks left and for the first two days we were left alone in the camp. During those two days the Hungarians with the white armbands again started to get busy [presumably they started to organise the camp], but everything was already chaotic. Work in the kitchens came to a halt, work in the offices and the workshops stopped. People rushed to the barbed wire fences and cut through them. They passed through them and made for the food stores in order to grab something to eat. No one left the camp even though they could have done so. Where could we go? We knew that we were deep in Germany and no one knew what was happening outside. In any case, 90 per cent of the people were unable to move as they were weak and sick.

On another day we already saw people in the camp who had changed into other clothes which were taken from the warehouses, and which were cleaner and in a better state. People began also to carry food which was taken from the stores. I decided to get out and to take at least something for me and my sister. In the square, people ran around as if they were possessed and carried whatever they could for themselves: food, clothes. The square was littered with the dead who were stepped on. No one looked around, everyone was absorbed by own needs. The healthy men and women organised tents in the square, and there they created sleeping facilities. Next to the tents they made fires and set up various metal containers in order to be able to cook something. It looked like a large gypsy camp. There were hundreds of such fires set in the fields, burning and smoking.

It was three days before the real liberation came. On 18 April 1945 a unit of the English Red Cross arrived in the camp. Cooking began in the kitchens, and late at night we received the first cooked food from the Red Cross. It was a dish of thick rice cooked with a lot of fat. Already, on the following day we received hot and very sweet milk, jam, and most importantly, meat and a hearty soup.

Several military personnel dressed in rubber clothing, masked and wearing rubber gloves on their hands came to us in the barrack. All the people in the bunks and around us in the whole block were sprayed with some sort of powder, from which all the vermin on us, the bugs and the lice, were immediately killed. We were finally freed of the lice which had been eating us alive. Doctors went around the barracks, asked us various questions and distributed all sorts of medicines.

A few days later in the camp, there was an outbreak of stomach typhus and dysentery.

With the passage of time they managed to empty out one of the barracks and to transfer the very sick into ambulances, those who had developed high temperatures. I was also taken away. They undressed me completely, wrapped me in a cover and took me away on a stretcher and placed me in an ambulance. The sick were washed thoroughly and changed into other clothes, and they let us lie on the stretchers until they organised bunks with soft bedding for each one. Nurses took care of us, gave us various medications and tonics to strengthen us.

The first night in the ambulance, I ran a very high temperature; I did not know what was happening around me. The following day I woke up, felt much better and asked for food. The doctor told me that during the night I had survived a crisis of stomach typhus. Later I began to feel a lot better. One morning my sister told me that she had good news for me. Immediately after that she brought in my younger brother Mendel, and a cousin, Avraham Biderman. There was a men's camp only a few kilometres from us where my brother and cousin had been. They were brought there a week before liberation. After they were liberated they went to the women's camp and asked after me and my sister. They went from block to block asking whether anyone knew of the two Blicblau sisters. In one of the blocks they met a woman who had come together with us from Mülhausen to Bergen-Belsen and she directed them to the block where my sister was to be found. This is how they found us and, together, came to me in the hospital.

A few days later my brother again visited me and informed me that he and the cousin, and in general all the men from his block, were being sent elsewhere, to Ciele, near Hanover, approximately thirty kilometres from Bergen-Belsen. He shared this with me so that I should know where to find him. Afterwards my sister came to tell me that she too was going somewhere else. All the healthy people from the camp were being transferred elsewhere. I didn't want to part from my sister and decided to go with her. I told her to bring me something to wear, and without waiting for the doctor I left the hospital and went with my sister to a camp a few kilometres further from this place, where we remained until coming here.

In this new camp, houses with wonderful rooms had been built. This was at one time a camp for the Hitler Youth, and not far from there was one of the palaces which was owned by Goering.[10] The rooms were clean and furnished. We were settled very comfortably. Six women were placed in my room, which was large.

In time all the people were moved from their previous places in Bergen-Belsen camp and sent to better and more comfortable places. The old camp was set alight and burned. All that remained of it was a heap of ashes, broken and burnt wire fences, a chimney from the crematoria and five mass graves in which rest the bones of 3000 people who were in the camp earlier, or who had died immediately after liberation when the English arrived in Bergen-Belsen.

More about Tobcia Blicblau

Tobcia Blicblau, a Holocaust survivor who passed away on 19 September 2018, gave her testimony to YIVO in 1949. She was born in Lodz on 19 May 1928 and her life in Lodz within a large family that included four siblings was relatively happy until the arrival of the Germans. Her father, Dovid Leib Blicblau, was a 'chazzan' (cantor) at the 'shul' (synagogue) that they attended, but he made his living from a butchery which he owned. He loved music and their home was filled with the sound of various musical instruments being played as he sang traditional songs. Chaya Frimet, Tobcia's mother, was a loving and gentle person and worked in a factory to bolster their income. This was all destroyed by the Nazis when they occupied Lodz and the horrors of the Holocaust were inflicted upon the family.

In the Lodz ghetto the family suffered from terrible hunger. Children were sent to work for the occupiers for half-days, every day, repairing fabrics, while the men worked in various factories. Her father, however, managed to be appointed as caretaker of the building in which they lived. This gave him the opportunity to appoint his wife as his assistant, which spared her from the harsh working conditions in the factories where she would have had to work under the gaze of an overseer. When her mother fell ill, Tobcia's brother managed to obtain medication for her illegally. Tobcia witnessed many German atrocities in the ghetto, such as the hanging of three Jews; however, as a child she wasn't aware of the reason for their death sentence. She often had to queue for food but was not always successful in obtaining it. Perhaps surprisingly, despite the appalling conditions in the ghetto, the Jews conducted reviews and plays in a theatre, and Tobcia indicated that she had been lucky enough to attend one performance. These performances assisted in boosting morale in the ghetto among the starving, tortured population.

Much of the following information about Tobcia's life was recounted to me by her niece Lane (also known as Tal) Schmerling, who lives in Melbourne.

Tobcia's brother Shlomo volunteered to work in Germany, believing that conditions would be better there. After four months in Germany he was transported back to Lodz, where he was imprisoned together with 350 other men. On 20 May 1941 he was transported again during the night. The family never found out where he was sent and he was never seen again. He was twenty years old at the time.

On 12 September 1942, the last day of the big 'Aktion' (a round-up of Jews to be transported to a camp), Tobcia, fourteen years old at the time, was rounded up in the courtyard of their house in the ghetto at 8 Lagiewnicka Street. She was placed on a horse-drawn cart which was to take her and others to waiting SS trucks. Mendel, her brother, jumped onto the cart and persuaded Tobcia to leap off together with him. They escaped into the depths of the ghetto, where they successfully hid until the Aktion was over. If not for Mendel's courage and quick thinking, she would have been taken to the death camp Chelmno. Their reprieve was tragically short-lived; the SS issued a notice that the ghetto was to be liquidated, and that the remaining inhabitants would be resettled elsewhere. The SS always used means to deceive the Jews into cooperating with them, because the victims believed that they would be better off in the new place. This enabled the SS to control the Jews without having to cope with panic and disorder. The Jewish police aided in the round-up and deportation of their brethren. The Jews were told to take with them precious documents and photos and little luggage. On 16 August 1944, Tobcia and her parents and siblings, Rosia and Lipman, were taken to Radegast Station in Lodz from which to be transported to an unknown destination. They were each given a loaf of bread for the journey, and they felt that this was worth its weight in gold! The train travelled from Lodz to Auschwitz-Birkenau. There Tobcia was separated from her parents: her mother's last words to her were 'Toybele, you're not fourteen, you're sixteen.' She clearly knew that sixteen-year-old youngsters would be taken for slave labour, giving them the chance to survive, whereas younger children would be sent to the gas chambers. Tobcia did not know that this was the last time she would see her parents. From then on she stopped smiling and crying. Her emotions seemed to be frozen in time.

Both Tobcia and her sister Rosia were incarcerated in Auschwitz-Birkenau from 16 August 1944 until they were moved once more. They both received prisoner numbers, but did not have them tattooed on their arms. The barrack in which they were housed was a long structure in which there were three-tiered bunks, each bunk for twelve inmates. They slept with six others lying in one direction, while the remaining six women slept with their heads on the opposite side. The inmates were primarily from Lodz. There was also a stove in the barrack used mainly by the block elder and the kapos. In addition there was a trough with one tap for washing themselves. Their routine was unvarying: three times per day the inmates had to stand outside in rows of five to be counted. Once a day soup was distributed by the block elder who would sometimes pour the soup on the ground if the inmates pushed too much. After five days, they were given a blanket each. While waiting for the blankets to be distributed, Tobcia found some relatives from outlying shtetls [villages]. Atop some of the buildings, high chimneys were emitting foul-smelling black smoke twenty-four hours a day. Tobcia asked some Ukrainian and Polish women what was being burned. Their reply was that Jewish people including Tobcia's parents were being incinerated.

Once again they were to be moved, on 24 August 1944, but before the journey began the prisoners were bathed and given a striped dress and wooden clogs. The women were deliberately given the wrong size garment in order to humiliate them, the tall wearing a short dress, the short wearing a long dress, and they had to scramble to exchange their clogs with other prisoners for a nearer fit. The journey by cattle truck to Ravensbruck women's forced labour camp took two days and two nights. The days were stiflingly hot and the nights were very cold. They were given no food or water, and had to use buckets as toilets.

These soon overflowed onto the floor of the truck, creating a terrible stench. Their destination was Mülhausen, a forced labour camp near Thüringen, Germany. The camp was established in the midst of a large forest for the production of arms for the Wehrmacht. Tobcia was put to work in an ammunitions factory, making timers for V1 and V2 bombs. Each labourer worked on a specific part of the mechanism and Tobcia's job was to file screws. Hanging was the punishment for sloppy work. The prisoners walked from the barrack to work in rows of five women. They were accompanied by German guards with dogs. In winter it was very difficult to walk in the snow. They started work at seven in the morning and were supervised by an SS guard. They were given coffee and bread at work, and soup and bread when they returned from work. They did not have to work on Sundays, and were given a special ration of a sausage or jam. Tobcia found the conditions and treatment at Mülhausen bearable, especially when contrasted to Auschwitz.

The block in which they were housed was shared by gypsies and it was not always a peaceful relationship. The bunks for sleeping were two tiered and the prisoners slept only two in a bunk. Tobcia and Rosia had a bunk to themselves – this was indeed luxury. They had a toilet and washbasin in the barrack which was cleaned regularly by a Jewish prisoner. Once per week they were allowed to take a bath, and have their clothes cleaned. As the women's hair began to grow, they began to feel more human, their self-esteem being partly restored under the more humane treatment. The Germans acceded to Tobcia's request for wool and knitting needles for the purpose of knitting gloves after work for the SS. She received an extra ration of bread for this service. Tobcia maintained that Rosia always cared for her, thus helping her to survive.

On 15 February 1945, Tobcia and other women were taken by truck to the camp Bergen-Belsen. Tobcia was filled with horror when they arrived at the camp. Despite all her suffering in other camps, she described Bergen-Belsen as 'hell on earth' when compared to anything she had encountered previously. The blocks were very cramped, with four women sharing a single bunk. The passage between the bunks was very narrow and difficult to negotiate. The barrack was filthy; a few taps supplied water, but not enough for the prisoners to wash themselves. Food and water ran out. People were skeletal, and suffered in agony from the bitter cold. They had no respite from the lice with which they were infested.

Pessy, a woman from Czechoslovakia, was put in charge of the barrack and she took a cruel pleasure in beating the women over the head with a stick. The chimneys continuously belched out a column of putrid black smoke.

For about ten days Tobcia had to work in a factory where slave labourers worked at cutting rags into long pieces which they then plaited as mats. Following her spell in the factory, she was made to dig trenches in the ground which had to be filled up the following day. The work was designed not only to exhaust the workers, but also to humiliate and demoralise them. Later, with her bleeding and blistered hands, Tobcia had to help chop down trees which were then dragged to the camp. In the camp the labourers were forced to place the wood in rows and then to stack bodies on top. In this way, they had to build a huge pyre which consisted of wood piles that alternated with bodies. The Germans set fire to the pyre, attempting to obliterate the evidence of their atrocities.

Every day the prisoners stood outside in the Appel place from 5.00am until 9.00am to be counted by the Germans repeatedly. Daily there were corpses that had to be removed from the barrack and placed with the living for counting so that figures would be correct according to German records.

Tobcia and Rosia were liberated by the British army on 15 April 1945. The Germans had disappeared from the camp before the British forces arrived. At the time, Tobcia was very ill, as were many others in the barrack. The English soldiers treated her gently, wrapping her in a blanket and transferring her by stretcher to a block which had been cleaned and fumigated, and made to serve as a makeshift hospital. The patients slept on straw mattresses on the floor, but they were supplied with sheets. Two Polish women were assigned to wash Tobcia, but they deliberately handled her very roughly, aggravating a wound which she had on her leg and calling her 'bloody Jewess' and other derogatory epithets.

Rosia was still in the women's camp at Bergen-Belsen, while Mendel and Avraham were in the men's camp. After liberation they came to the women's camp to search for relatives who might have survived and they found Rosia and Tobcia, whom they were unable to recognise because Tobcia was in such poor physical condition. After a few days, Rosia arrived at the hospital to inform Tobcia that she was being moved to another camp. Tobcia left the hospital, stealing a dress to wear when she and Rosia left the camp. They had survived the Holocaust together and were not willing to be parted at any cost. They found a Displaced Persons camp, where they were accommodated and assigned to a room containing two bunks, a table and a stove. Although the room and its contents were rudimentary, it was a sanctuary for the two women after they had been incarcerated for so long. In December a school was established in the DP camp, run by men from the Jewish Brigade whose service in the British army in Palestine had come to an end.

Tobcia immediately started to study and she learned Hebrew, which was to stand her in good stead in the future when she emigrated to Israel. There was grieving and rejoicing as more relatives found each other, but Tobcia's traumatic experiences during the Holocaust left her scarred emotionally for the remainder of her life. Tobcia and her siblings received help from the Joint to enable them to travel to Australia. Entry visas had been arranged by the Rosenfeld family, who had been their neighbours in Lodz. Sailing on the ship *Ville D'Amiens* from Marseilles, she arrived in Melbourne on 19 July 1947, together with her brother Lipman.

Lipman, Mendel and Tobcia shared a small one-room apartment which Mendel purchased with a loan from the Jewish Welfare Society. Their new home was in Beaconsfield Parade, St Kilda. Many of the Jewish refugees started their new lives in this way, helped by Jewish organisations such as the Jewish Welfare Society. Superficially at least, it seemed that the obstacles and difficulties of having to adjust to an alien culture were overcome by the majority of the new arrivals who showed remarkable resilience and determination. However, many of them remained haunted by their appalling experiences in German-occupied Europe. Tobcia was profoundly affected by her experiences; despite this, her ambition to build a better life sustained her as she pursued her goals. She was bright, ambitious and determined. She spoke fluent Yiddish, Polish and German, and a smattering of Hebrew. She was not shy about expressing her opinions, sometimes too forcefully. She chatted easily to people of different ages, always kept up with current affairs, and could be very engaging in conversation.

Within a few days of landing in Australia, Tobcia found work in a factory, and then continued to do the same work for about nine years. She was determined to improve her life and she attended night classes to learn English, following which she used her skills to complete two courses in Ladies Advanced Cutting and Design for dresses, skirts, sportswear and lingerie at Bradshaw's Business College in Melbourne in 1951. She also studied Business and Calculator Operating in 1962. As well, the college provided courses for returning servicemen who had recently returned from Europe.

Tobcia's next foray into the workplace was with the Australian Jewish Welfare and Relief Society at 466 Punt Road, South Yarra, where she worked as a receptionist from 1957 to 1964. Another of her tasks was to 'meet and greet' passengers from the ships that brought Jewish survivors to Australian shores. Her own experience and her knowledge of languages made her a natural choice for the work. In 1954, she began to teach Yiddish at the I.L. Peretz Yiddish School and Kindergarten in Carlton. Tobcia never married, but family life for her was rich and filled with affection from her siblings and their families. Nieces and nephews seemed to fill any void she may have felt in not having her own children.

Despite this family life, Tobcia was beginning to feel that Melbourne was no longer fulfilling her needs, so she decided to emigrate to Israel in 1964 where she was offered a position in the Australian Embassy. Her responsibilities and range of duties varied and she enjoyed the variety, but when in 1988 she reached the age of sixty, which was the statutory retirement age then, she had to stop work. She continued to enjoy life in Israel until, once again, she felt the need to be closer to the Australian family members after a number of her relatives in Israel had passed away. She left Israel in 2007 after having spent forty-three years in the country. Her restlessness, her innate sense of loneliness, was never fully appeased and she went on searching for the contentment that constantly eluded her. Her dedicated search for education, her interest in world affairs, never brought her lasting comfort. She always felt aggrieved, and that she was not appreciated.

Her return to Australia in March 2007 could have been a happy event if Tobcia had not begun to feel that she did not receive the attention and love from her nieces and nephews that she sought. She did not show any joy at their efforts and frequently found much to complain about. Her niece Tal Schmerling observed that Tobcia used to say that she often saw survivors who lived happy and fulfilling lives having children, and happy families, and she could not understand how they did it after what they went through in the Holocaust. Contentment always eluded her, but she was perceptive enough to understand that she should have sought psychiatric help after she first arrived in Australia. She added that at that time people assumed that psychiatric help was only for the 'crazies'. Tal further observed that 'Tobcia's experiences impacted her severely, both physically and emotionally. She never forgave God for the crimes committed against her, her family and her community. I don't think she ever forgave humanity'[11] for their perpetuation of evil in the world.

THE JEWISH POLICE IN PLASZOW GHETTO

Maria Roza Kamsler

In March 1941 the entire Jewish population of Krakow was locked into the ghetto. For seven months, from March until October 1941, my family managed to sustain themselves in a village outside the ghetto. After that, when it was forbidden for Jews to live outside the ghetto, we returned to Krakow. We lived there until the expulsion. My parents were sent away with the first transports in June 1942. I was sent away later – in January 1943.

The first transport included all the Jews who did not have work in a German factory. SS personnel surrounded the ghetto and carried out an inspection of all kenkarten [identity documents]. When someone found work, that person received a stamp on his card. Those who did not have this verification were held on the spot and sent to the assembly point. Right from the start my parents were aware of the likelihood of their being transported, and one day the total number of people whom the Germans had assigned to join a specific transport was short of the required number. They then laid siege to whole streets, closed them off and carried out house searches. During such a house search they took away my parents. Where they sent them, what happened to them, where they vanished to, I don't know until this very day.

The second transport took place in October 1942. At that time they sent away my closest remaining family members who had also lived in the ghetto, and I was left completely alone.

In the ghetto I was assigned to work for the Germans in the feldzug dienststelle [battle service armoury] factories where guns were repaired: rifles, revolvers and even cannons. For a certain time I worked in the section where they tested the repaired guns – rifles and revolvers – testing them to see whether they functioned properly, and whether or not the shot hit the target accurately. Later, I worked at cleaning the repaired guns. At that time, the Germans still paid wages for work, but the sum was minimal. One week's wages lasted for one or two days even though I lived modestly. I improved my situation by gradually selling possessions which had been left in our house after my parents were transported.

In the vicinity of the Krakow ghetto there existed a secret resistance movement. I do not know when the resistance organisation was established. In any case, the formation of this specific organisation might have arisen because of the persecution which we had to endure in the ghetto itself, and also perhaps because of the persistent belief in the rumours which had spread long ago in the ghetto that Jews were being sent to their death, that there were special death camps – news that we did not believe at first. It appeared that there was nothing more to lose and it was agreed that we should organise ourselves to resist the Germans.

I personally was a member of this organisation. I was drawn into it by a girl whose name was Ada (I don't remember her family name) with whom I worked, and with whom I eventually became friends. Ada worked in the garden of the factory. I worked in a section of the shooting range where the guns were tested. Every day at noon we would meet. One day she suggested to me that I should surreptitiously put aside bullets, little by little, and every day, in an arranged spot not far from the range, the bullets would be passed on to her. According to what she told me, the bullets were taken into the ghetto where a portion went to the resistance [inside the ghetto], and a portion went to the Polish resistance outside the ghetto.

The theft of the bullets went on for about three months, for as long as I worked in the section where the guns were tested. Later when I began to work at cleaning the guns inside the factories, I stole and removed gun parts: springs and parts in which there are the pins which discharge the bullets. I also undertook to give these parts to Adan [a resistance group]. This continued until I was incarcerated. In the ghetto I had a whole group of young friends with whom I had become acquainted. They too were members of the resistance organisation, but I did not know about it at the time. It was only when the group was compromised and they were all arrested and shot that I became aware of this. This incident was widely discussed in the ghetto. The person who betrayed them was a member of the group. He was named Mietek. I don't remember his family name.

In January 1943, all those who worked for the Germans in the factories were ordered to move to the barracks located near Plaszow which was a suburb of Krakow, to live there, and from there to travel to work every day. The barracks were built in the area of the Jewish cemetery in Plaszow. The cemetery was cleared for this purpose and the ground later became unrecognisable as a former cemetery.

Plaszow was a labour camp. There were about 1000 people incarcerated there, men and women, all from Krakow. The camp was managed by the Jewish police. The camp chief was an SS man, Amon Goeth, who was captured after the war and hanged [for having committed war crimes]. A number of the people living in Plaszow camp worked 'in situ', building barracks and various canals. Among the prisoners there were many who died at that time. During the daily inspection, the Kommandant of the camp, Goeth, would use various pretexts to shoot a few people.

The ghetto in Krakow was liquidated in March 1943 and a large number of people from there were brought to Plaszow. They were mostly slave labourers. According to what I heard, others were liquidated in the ghetto itself or sent to the death camps.

In April 1943, the gun factory where I had worked all the time was closed down gradually. I too lost my job. Thus I decided to run away from Plaszow. Being locked up permanently in the camp influenced my decision to run away, because for as long as I was working, I had contact with the outside world, life was bearable, and I was not tempted to take risks such as running away which would endanger my life. Thereafter, I made the decision to do so. I had a Christian acquaintance, Vizhnievska, who had worked with me in the factory. At one point she said to me that if I should want to escape, she would help me to hide on the Aryan side. On the day that we went from the factory to Plaszow for the last time, I left my work kommando [unit] and hid myself near a gateway. However, a Jewish policeman noticed this and ran to me advising me to return to my group, because he was responsible for each person who might go missing and he would pay for my escape with his head. I had no choice but to return to my group. It was clear to me that if I did not do this willingly, he would take me by force and report me to a German soldier. They would have shot or hanged me immediately.

On the following day I was assigned to work at road building and in sewerage maintenance. I worked with a group which completed a road of sorts. Goeth issued an order that the road must be completed within a particular period. Since the order was not fulfilled despite our efforts, he punished our group with beatings. We were all lined up and Goeth passed by us selecting victims for punishment. Several tables were brought out on which we were to be beaten. Men had to take down their trousers – women, their underwear – and they were beaten on their bare chests. Those who carried out the punishment were Ukrainians who used carters' whips. In addition, the victim himself or herself had to count the lashes. The minimum number of lashes was at least fifty. After the punishment was executed, the victims themselves had to collect their clothes, put them in order, and then, bloodied and beaten, they had to place themselves in rows. Those who fainted during the beating were revived by means of buckets of cold water poured over their lashed bodies.

A few days later I was made kapo in control of a group of twenty-eight women. That group worked at carrying buckets of water to pour into a machine which crushed stones for concreting the road. I did not work for long with that group. Within a week I became ill. I was placed in the hospital and afterwards I was even given three free rest days before I returned to work. A Jewish policeman noticed me on the third day as I wandered around the camp doing nothing. He took me to the headquarters of the Jewish police in order for me to clean the building. While I was cleaning, the chief of the Jewish police was there, Wilhelm Chilowitz, a Jew from Krakow who had enormous powers over the camp inhabitants. He was able to send people to their deaths, to be burned, or to allocate them to the sort of work within the camp itself which quickly killed them.

Wilhelm Chilowitz, or 'Wilek', as he was called, came from the Krakow underworld. He was a brutal man and a wastrel. The inhabitants of the camp feared and hated him. When people from the Krakow ghetto were brought to the camp, first of all they were robbed, and whatever possessions or money they carried with them was expropriated for the chief. The looting was carried out by the Jewish policemen under the supervision of Chilowitz. He accumulated a large fortune from these activities, taking much of the proceeds for himself. He had links with the German Kommandant, Goeth, and together they carried out various despicable acts.

Chilowitz would roam around the camp with a carter's whip in his hand, and he would lash anyone for the smallest transgression. But his end was gruesome: he was later shot by Goeth himself. When I was at work in the police office, Chilowitz informed me that I could continue to work there if they were satisfied with my work. Someone else who had worked there before me was transferred to another labour camp in the Zablocie region near Krakow.

I worked in the police office for approximately six months. I knew that Chilowitz looked for good opportunities to be with women in the camp. He had a large enough choice. During his many affairs with women, he had to extricate himself from all sorts of jealous scenes with his wife, Marisha, who also worked in the Jewish police force. In addition, she was on very good terms with Goeth and was able to cause a lot of trouble for people she wished to punish. There were incidents when she took revenge on the women who had liaisons with her husband. She had many of those women sent to the extermination camps. For this reason alone it was very dangerous to have contact with her.

While I was working in the Jewish police offices, I made an effort not to give Chilowitz or his co-workers any opportunity to get close to me. Of particular relief for me in this regard was the fact that Chilowitz and his wife knew me from the ghetto in Krakow. For some time the Chilowitzes had lived in the same building as we did. Chilowitz spared me somewhat. I was also lucky with Chilowitz's wife who treated me very well. A number of satirical songs about Chilowitz were composed in the camp. I do not recall all of them. A few fragments have remained in my memory. The songs written in Polish were composed by a girl whose name I no longer remember. She was punished for this by Chilowitz who had her placed in a cell for several days. The songs were very popular in the camp. The whole camp knew the songs and sang them when the opportunity arose. There was also someone who wrote satirical songs in Yiddish. I remember some of those songs. The following song is about Kerner, the Jewish police officer, in the camp:

> *Meir Kerner, the rogue*
> *Does not know what he is doing.*
> *Tomorrow he will lie in a good place.*

There were many brutal and sadistic people to be found among the Jewish police. In this regard, two officers, Kernen and Finkelstein, stood out separately. Kernen was fond of whipping with his carter's whip. His favourite place to aim for with the whip was the eyes. I saw how the police whipped the naked bodies of two young boys because they had stolen a few potatoes. Their screams were chilling, and the more they screamed, the harder they were beaten.

The subject of the general sexual life in the camp is another chapter altogether. Basically, meetings between men and women were forbidden. Men and women could get together only at specific times of the day outdoors. It was not allowed for them to meet in the barracks, but their instincts prevailed over all dangers. Men came to women and women came to men. Frequently one would even stay overnight with the other one and in the presence of other people – men or women – they had sexual relations without shame. The police were responsible for supervision, but in this regard they could be influenced. They 'looked through their fingers' at what was going on. For the German authorities these things 'never happened'. In this situation there was no one who objected.

Many women willingly and gladly had sexual relations with the Jewish police. They enjoyed different privileges as payment. A policeman in this position always gave his woman something and also paid her with food or clothing.

There were many cases of abortion in the camp hospital. If a woman was far gone in her pregnancy, she was taken to the hospital to have the foetus aborted. This had to be done in great secrecy, because officially Jews were not allowed to have any sexual relations. A Jewish woman was forbidden to become pregnant. This was punishable by death. But there was a Jewish doctor in the camp hospital who helped out many who were in this state.

After working as a cleaner in the Jewish police quarters for about six months, I was sent to do other work [in a different camp]. This was when many of the camp inmates were sent to work in Skarszysko and Pianki. There was a chemical factory in Skarszysko. People did not last long doing this work [working with chemicals], becoming sick from the gases and various chemicals with which they came in contact. People turned yellow from the work, and contracted tuberculosis or some other fatal disease. In Pianki there was an alcohol factory. I was not sent away; instead I was assigned to the kitchen service to peel potatoes. I was engaged in this work until January 1944. It was hard. I had to peel four large buckets of potatoes every day and the potatoes were very small, rotten and dirty. Hence I had an opportunity to steal potatoes, not only for my personal use, but also to sell to others and to receive money or bread in exchange.

In January 1944, I was placed in the tailoring factory in the camp. There military uniforms were repaired. There was absolutely no chance of doing 'left' [illegal] business in the factory. We worked there for twenty-four hours divided into two shifts. Every shift worked for two weeks during the day, and for two weeks during the night. There was no rest day including Sunday. The work itself was not difficult, but the conditions were awful. The twelve-hour shifts were very tiring, especially without a Sunday rest. In addition, conditions in the camp were generally difficult at the time. The camp was completely cut off from the outside world and it was impossible to buy anything even with money or valuables.

In April 1944 I was sent away from the camp. I was taken to Krakow where I worked in the metal factory, 'German Enamel Works', in Zablace. Enamel pots and detonators for grenades were manufactured in the factory.[1]

This section describes, in some detail, the Plaszow camp and its inner workings. I belonged to a small group of people who were exceptions. For example, I was fortunate that I had worked as a cleaner in the Jewish police offices for a long time which enabled me to avoid different dangers in the camp itself. Many others – perhaps the majority – were not so fortunate. It was a daily occurrence in the camp that people were shot for no reason at all. Someone was shot because five guilders were found on him. A Jewish boy was shot because he whistled a Russian tune. The name of that particular boy was Tobcianshtok; I think he was from Krakow. A work kommando in the camp laboured at carrying bricks and wooden boards. SS men would often amuse themselves with this group by shooting them while they were carrying the bricks and boards.

In the tailoring workshop where I had worked, there were instances where people were shot while they were at their work-tables. This would happen mostly at night. The German overseer would peer in through the workshop window in order to see if work was being done. It sometimes happened that a worker would doze off at his work from exhaustion and weariness, and if he were caught sleeping, he would immediately receive a bullet in the head. The workers would try to protect one another, and see that no one fell asleep, but it was impossible to do so successfully. People were so exhausted and weary that they worked like automatons.

A rare occurrence took place in the camp: it concerned a Jewish girl who had an intimate relationship with one of the SS men. The SS man was in love with her. For a long time it was a big secret, no one knew about it. But unfortunately for the girl she broke her arm. Because of this incident, the SS man paid her excessive attention. His interest in her fate was conspicuous. The matter was looked into and the whole affair was revealed. In accordance with an order from the German powers, the SS man himself had to shoot the girl, together with her brother who was with her in the camp.

I worked in the factory at Zablace until the end of August 1944. Approximately 1000 people worked there. The work was very difficult but living conditions were not too bad, and the treatment was bearable. The chief of the work camp was an SS man. His aides were German civilians and Jewish police. The five months that I worked there were in any case comparatively quiet. In approximately August 1944 an order for the closure of the labour camp was issued. It was later evacuated further to the West. We were all sent back to Plaszow. Ironically we arrived there during a transport. Plaszow too was evacuated and the inhabitants were sent to various camps in Germany – Buchenwald and others. During the course of several days almost all the prisoners were sent out. A small group of people remained behind, most of them women. I too remained in the camp. Only a few hundred out of the 20,000 people who had been in the camp were left. Our group was there until October 1944.

Sadly, a great many people died in Plaszow. There were no longer any Jewish policemen there. Most Jewish officials were also transported, and those that remained played no role in the camp. Their place was taken by newly arrived Germans, civilian Germans. Even Chilowitz, the former chief of the Jewish police and Goeth's first aide, no longer had any role. A few weeks later his life was taken: Goeth himself shot Chilowitz. At the same time, he shot six of Chilowitz's closest family: his wife Marisha, Chilowitz's helper, the police officer Finkelstein and another three of his relatives who were also in the camp – the Ferber family from Krakow. It was said that they were shot for various transgressions. All six people who were shot were laid out in the middle of the camp road, and nearby was placed a large sign written in German and Polish: 'Shot while attempting to escape, owning firearms, having money and possessions.' After the Appel all of us were lined up in rows and led past the corpses in order to show us their fate.

In the camp there was a great deal of discussion about this, especially the fact that Goeth had shot Chilowitz and his family because they were no longer of any use to him, and he wanted to get rid of them because they knew too much about Goeth's secret business affairs. At the same time five Jewish youths who were brought from Vilcica were hanged. They worked in the Vilcica salt mine. When the camp there was liquidated, the youths attempted to hide. They were caught, brought to Plaszow and hanged. In the morning we saw how a gallows was set up in the square. This indicated that they would hang someone today. Who would hang – how many – this was something that no one could know. After the execution and the Appel at night before we retired, we were all taken in rows past the gallows where they showed us the five hanged youths.

I was assigned to work in the disinfection section of the camp. I deloused barracks, disinfected clothes, underwear and bedding. I had another occupation: fat, living bed-bugs were collected and put into glass containers, so that various experiments about their ability to withstand different gases could be carried out. While working in the disinfection unit, I had the opportunity to earn a little money. I had access to various goods, clothes, underwear and bedding which I was able to steal. I only needed someone to take the goods out of the camp in order to sell them. A girl from Krakow, Rutke Filer, whom I met in the camp and with whom I became friendly, helped me considerably in this respect. Rutke Filer worked with a group which exited the camp every day to work somewhere behind the town, and each time they went to work, she would take a few things with her to sell. We shared the earnings. We did not accept money for the sold goods, but food such as bread and butter, as well as cigarettes and other things. With food to eat, I did not live at all badly during that time.

In October a significant number of people out of the few hundred in Plaszow were sent away. Suddenly in the middle of the night an Appel was carried out, during which a long list of names were read out, including my name. Immediately after the Appel we were sent to the train, loaded onto wagons, and we began to move. We travelled for a day and a night after which the train stopped. Amid a clamour and a din, and wild shouts from SS men, we were driven out of the wagons.

During the whole journey no one knew our destination. Immediately we alighted, we saw a sign with the following writing: Auschwitz. We knew the meaning of Auschwitz from having heard about it earlier in other camps. We did not step out onto the actual train station, but into the camp itself, where there was a railway line. The first thing that they did was to take us to the showers. It was nighttime, dark, one could see only the wire fencing around the darkened buildings. But we could smell a strange stench, a smell of burnt objects. The air was saturated with the acrid smoke and the smell of burning. We were led into a large hall in a walled-in building. The hall was filled with women. It was crowded, hot and stifling. We remained there all night. No one approached us and none of us knew what would be done with us later. People made jokes in their bitterness: [such as] we would be showered and afterward, clean, we would be sent to the gas chamber. Thus the night passed. We sat there for a whole day and another night.

At dawn the door opened and several SS men entered. We were told to undress completely and to place ourselves in a line. When we were standing naked and in line, a doctor entered together with several SS men. Every woman had to pass in front of them and each of us was looked at from top to toe. Women who were old or had a poor physique, or who had even the slightest defect, or the least bit of dirt on their body, were held back, left in the hall. All the rest were allowed to go through. I too was among those whom the doctor permitted to go into the other room. There our hair was again cut, shorn down to the roots, and the hair of all other parts of the body except for the head was very thoroughly removed. This work was carried out by Hungarian and Czechoslovakian Jewish women. Those women did their work very brutally, beating and hitting us for the smallest motion. They took no care when they worked with razors to remove hair from the intimate parts of the body. When they left the 'hair-salon' many women were bleeding. Afterwards we were taken to the shower. A burst of cold water gushed down on us and after a few minutes, wet and soaked through, feverish from the wet and the cold, we were taken to another room where we were given clothes. The clothes were suitable for a costume party: tall women received short dresses, short ones were given very long dresses. The dresses were made of silk-like material, very thin garments. We did not receive any underwear, and for our feet we were given wooden clogs to wear; in this way, not yet dry and with our heads wet, and wearing damp dresses, we were taken immediately to an open field. It was the middle of October and it was already very cold. Night had fallen and we remained in the field for several hours. An SS man arrived later and took us, barefoot, to Birkenau camp (Auschwitz had a complex of camps, many kilometres in length and width, and Birkenau was part of the camp-complex).

A barrack elder [a woman] was already waiting in front of the Birkenau camp. She was assigned to us. The block elder was a Hungarian Jewish woman. She took over from the SS man, led us to the barrack which looked like a stable: on both sides of the walls there were three-tiered planks [for sleeping purposes] and there was a passage between them. At dawn, at about five o'clock, frightful shouts woke us up. We got up from the bunks, stepped onto the floor, and went for coffee. Each of us received a little pot of black, bitter coffee. Two hours later we were led to the Appel. We were chased by the block elder's helpers – all of them were Hungarian Jewish women. Not only did they shout, but they beat us with sticks. The Appel lasted for a few hours and afterwards we were sent back to the barrack. For a week long, we had to put up with pointless Appels, twice a day for several hours. A week later an

SS man arrived at our block and selected a group of women. He chose those that were good-looking, and rejected the others.

Myself and Rutke Filer were among those who were chosen by the Germans and taken to another block. At night they took us to be tattooed. Women did this work. On the last portion [end] of the first half of the left hand, close to the wrist, a number was tattooed, followed by a letter from the alphabet. My number is '26345 A'. The earlier tattoos did not have an alphabetical letter, only a number. Those who were brought to Auschwitz in 1944 did have a letter 'A' after the number. Later the letter 'B' followed all even numbers. It was stated that every 100,000 in a recorded year (1944) had a different letter. Also, these ciphers had very different meanings. The first two ciphers meant – the even number of the transport. The other letters meant the actual transport. My number means: series 'A', 26th transport, 345th, according to the transport data.

The tattooing went very quickly. It was done according to a routine and with great dexterity. Our whole group which consisted of 500 women was dealt with in one night. On the following day we were sent to 'P.K.L.' [Plaster Concentration Camp]. There we again had to shower and to have a medical examination. During the examination many women from our group were rejected. Rutke Filer and I were lucky to get through. This time we were soon given decent woollen dresses, sweaters and coats. We were sent to a camp several kilometres further away which was called: 'Auschwitz Men's Camp'. Two blocks were assigned to women. We were quartered there, and on a different day we were assigned some work. I belonged to the group 'Shtrasen-bau' (road building). It appeared that we were to carry stones, to use little wagons filled with sand and also to do other work. I worked there until January 1945. With the passing of time, a systematic liquidation of Auschwitz camps began to take place. No new people were brought there; on the contrary, every day transports left with people, and the number of those who remained became smaller all the time. On 18 January 1945 our camp was liquidated. With the exception of sick and a few healthy people, everyone was sent away. We were taken eastwards to Silesia. On the way we came across huge military encampments, soldiers and ammunition stores. It was evidently the German army withdrawal; at least the appearance of the military was good, disciplined.

We travelled for three days and three nights. Thousands and thousands of people were walking under the watch of the SS. Many people were shot on the way. Anyone who lagged behind, or was unable to continue, or who could not keep up the pace, was shot. The road was littered with the dead, those shot, on both sides of the highway.

On the third day we arrived in a Silesian village, Wodzislaw. There we were loaded onto coal wagons and we rode on the railway. We travelled for three days. The frost was terrible and many people froze on the way, dying from the cold. On the third day we arrived at Ravensbruck. We were located in a tent in an open field and we slept on the frozen earth. It was earth paved with stones and frozen filth which melted from the warmth of our bodies. In this camp there was total hunger. We received nothing to eat. There was terrible disorder, chaos. Here we encountered many women who had been there a long time. They were no longer human, but shadows of humans. Emaciated, skin and bones, dejected, they looked like walking skeletons.[2] Regular transports were sent from there too. At that time the Germans had no need to take people to the transports – people went of their own free will. Masses appeared willingly for every transport, and they themselves asked to be sent away, as life there [in Ravensbruck] was so bitter. Where they were being sent – the further the better – no one was any longer interested in a destination. People were already resigned, tired out, so exhausted that for everyone it made no difference what would happen later, far away, somewhere different, as long as it was away from the hellish situation in Ravensbruck.

I too was sent away on one of these transports. We were taken to Neustadt-Glewe where there was a small camp. There were many women there who were brought after the Warsaw uprising.

Conditions in this camp were no better than in Ravensbruck. We slept on the ground and food consisted of one kilogram of bread for ten people. Our work was to dig trenches for protection against air raids. Our camp was situated on the actual aerodrome. There were daily air battles and air combat. There we saw clearly what was happening on the fronts, that the German situation was bad, and that the end was near. Everyone had one desire: to hold on for a little longer until we would be released.

With every passing day the desire to live, to survive, to overcome, to see the end, became stronger. Morale improved and it became easier to withstand the difficulties, the bitter life in the camp. Right there, in Neustadt-Glewe, I survived until the hour of liberation. I was there until the end of the war, until 2 May 1945, when the Germans left and the first American troops showed up.

On the morning of 2 May, the normal Appel took place. However, immediately afterwards we noticed that a change was taking place in the camp, something extraordinary was happening: trucks had parked in front of the ammunitions storehouse and soldiers were hurriedly taking out and loading everything that was possible onto the lorries. Soon we became aware of an order that was given to German prisoners – criminals, thieves and prostitutes, who were also in the camp – to get ready to depart.

Events happened with lightning speed. A woman who worked in the camp office informed us that we would soon be free. She had heard the Germans discussing this and she made no secret of it. Everything was a question of hours or perhaps even minutes.

Suddenly, the Germans issued an order for all the camp inhabitants to return to the barracks and to remain there. Few dared to appear outdoors. The final moments were critical. Who knew what the Germans might do to the camp at the last minute. Many of the people in the camp did not follow the order. A group of women invaded the food stores, in order to help themselves to food from there. The Germans began to shoot at the women and a few of them were killed. After this happened, everyone returned to the barracks. We sat and waited. No one knew what was happening outside.

A noise started outside, a racket, but suddenly it became quiet, deathly quiet. This strange silence attracted attention. Someone dared to leave the barrack in order to take a look at what was happening outside. The Germans were no longer in the camp. The camp square was completely quiet. The camp watchtowers stood empty, desolate. A shout was heard: we are free! Everyone came out of the barracks.

Immediately people began to raid the food storerooms. Like starving wolves, people grabbed whatever they could eat. People were indescribably happy. They cried from happiness – of course they wept from the joy of having lived until the moment of liberation. Where does one find the words to describe the joyful picture that was reflected by everyone in that hour?

There was a stream of people at the camp square, all of who began to prepare something to eat, a cooked dish. People laid fires just like gypsies in a field, and there they placed pots in which they cooked food. It was already evening. It was quiet around us. Once we had eaten, we were exhausted, and worn out, we returned to the barracks to sleep. At dawn we left the barracks and went over to the SS buildings. They were clean and comfortable. There we organised ourselves into groups and afterwards we went to the town in our groups. We did not see any new military; none of the Allied armies had appeared yet. We had only got rid of the Germans. No one knew who was in the town nor what might happen there, but people went with abandonment, they could not hold themselves back. They were driven by the desire to get out of the camp to the external free world.

In the town we saw the first of the American military, but they drove past the town and did not stop. The town seemed to be dead. Many German families went deeper into the countryside with the army and deserted their houses and buildings. Those who remained were only old men, women and children. The streets were deserted; no Germans were to be seen as they were confined to their homes.

Men and women from the camp made a great noise as they wandered in groups all over the town. A wild feeling of hate, a desire for revenge, wanting to destroy and rob overcame everyone. Each of us was armed with an axe, a hammer or a bayonet which we found in the camp and even more were scattered all over the town in many streets. People destroyed the windows of the deserted houses, broke down doors, entered and searched every corner, hacked and broke furniture and glassware. Food and other things which were necessary or valuable were looted. The same thing occurred even in inhabited houses. There was no feeling of shared suffering, no response to entreaty and tears, no excuses or sympathy. We treated the Germans as they had treated us – brutally, crudely and heartlessly. Our wrath was not lessened by the sight of German tears while we were breaking and destroying, beating and robbing.

When we entered a house in which there were Germans, we heard our first order [from Russians]: 'Everyone stand to one side, not to move from the spot.' Together with our groups there were also Russian prisoners of war who had left their camp which was not far from the town. The Germans obediently followed the order, they met us with fear and loathing. We cursed them with obscenities, just as they had spoken to us only a day earlier, pushed, beat us down, hit us, as they had tortured us just the day before. German women begged us to have pity on them, not to rob them, complained that they were not guilty, that not one of them had belonged to the Nazi Party. In a moment they all became opposed to Hitler and his regime and distanced themselves from him. No one took any notice of the complaints and pleas. We searched and examined every corner, we smashed and destroyed, purloined food, clothes and possessions, and simply continued onwards.

When the pogrom in the town was over, we returned exhausted to the camp with our loot, and satisfied our hunger with the stolen food which was good and plentiful, but many people were unable to digest it as for a long time they had been deprived of such rich food. Their systems were weakened and many of them vomited it up, but soon thereafter they began to eat again. They responded to their renewed feeling of hunger.

On another day we again went to the town in order to kill and rob its environs. I, together with my group of women, entered a German agricultural site where they bred rabbits. We wanted to take a few for ourselves in order to slaughter and cook them in the camp. A German opposed us and began to shout and block our way. I stabbed him in the stomach with my knife. He fell down bleeding and yelling. His wife began to shout and cry. We ignored her cries, went into the hutch, took a few rabbits and carried on. We lived a chaotic life for several days, a life of revenge, destruction and robbery. During those few days, many American soldiers drove through the town, and later, Russian units. No one stopped there. The town was ignored and in a mess. In the meantime, no army remained there. Only we, the camp inhabitants, reigned there. But in the vicinity around the town the Russian military had stationed themselves. Once we even visited the Russian headquarters, where we were very well received. We helped with digging up potatoes for the army, worked at this for several hours, and thereafter we received a huge pack of food, conserves, pig-fat, other food and cigarettes, a pack which we barely managed to drag to the camp.

After about another week, the Russian army occupied the town officially, and they made one of the houses their headquarters. From that time onwards, our control of the town, the pogroms and the robbery stopped. The military restored peace and order. Every day the authorities supplied the camp people with various foods. But we accepted hardly any food, because we had enough in the camp. We had a generous amount of meat which was really good and also chicken. We took all the poultry from the town, brought it to the camp, and almost daily we ate cooked chicken.

We learned of the end of the war on 9 May. On that day we heard about the capitulation of the Germans. A Russian military parade of the units stationed there took place on a large square at the back of the town. The soldiers got drunk on that day and sang and danced. Many of our camp people left that place, but everyone was generously given drinks and nibbles. The soldiers and the camp people mixed joyfully together, ate and drank, sang and danced.

We celebrated in the camp where we ate and drank for approximately two weeks, lived without knowing what would happen in the future, what they would do with us and where we would go. Suddenly the Russians issued an order for us to clean the houses and barracks because they were needed for the army. This time the people moved from the place. Folks began to wander: we went in different directions. Russian women from the prison camps, Polish women, many of our Jewish women, went in the direction of their former homes – towards the east. French men and women, Belgians all went west, in the direction of their countries and homes. Jews went in several directions, both eastwards towards Poland, and westwards to the American zone which was situated not far from our town.

Also, my group of women from Poland took to the road. We loaded our goods onto a bicycle and a child's pram and we were off. We went eastwards in the direction of Krakow. We travelled for two weeks. The walking was very hard on us. We could not cover more than ten kilometres a day and we had a long and difficult way to go. On the way we slept in abandoned houses, in fields, and in the morning we continued. On the third day we came across a Russian army truck onto which all of us were loaded and taken to a large town. There the authorities provided us with a horse and cart with which we travelled further, together with a few Polish youngsters. We dragged on for more than a week before we arrived in Starograd. From there we travelled further on a fruit-train across Posen, then Katowice to Krakow.

What each of us experienced and felt when we arrived in our birthplace Krakow is difficult to describe. Krakow, my birthplace and home, where I grew up, seemed strange to me. I no longer had a home and no family to go to. The house where we had lived was sound and looked exactly as it had before the war. It had not changed at all – only inside the house were new people, new occupants. Where does one go? That was the first question that we asked one another. There was no one to go to. The only address for us was the Jewish Committee in Krakow. We went there and they gave us refuge in an international place for returnees. I remained there for several months and then I took up trading and I moved into a private home with a family. I traded in anything that I was able to as long as I could make a living from it. I took cigarettes from Krakow to Prague and went back with used clothing, and traded also in finance; in this way, alone, I supported myself until I moved to Australia.

More about Maria Roza Kamsler

Maria was born in Krakow, Poland. She was an only child born to adoring parents who lived comfortably at 3 Kaputshinska Street. Maria's father was tall and slim in build, vain about his appearance, and might be described as something of a dandy. He liked his shoes to be polished at all times, to be shiny and clean. He was ambitious and achieved some success in his business, a limestone mine. Maria was very attached to him, but she was particularly devoted to her grandmother, who was very affectionate and loving. Her grandfather, who was a butcher, lived in Butkow in Czechoslovakia, and Maria loved to holiday there during vacation time. The grandfather was called Jacob, and the grandmother's name was Roza.

Maria's future husband, Leon Brooks, who lived in Lodz, was about to be conscripted into the Polish army, but chose to leave Poland in order to avoid serving in the Polish military. Maria didn't know him in Poland, but in Melbourne they were introduced to each other by a friend. He arrived in Melbourne in 1937. Leon served in the Australian army and was posted to New Guinea, where he spent some time in hospital after having contracted a tropical disease. Among his experiences in Australia, he tried fruit-picking in Shepparton, a rich fruit-producing area, where he earned his living for a while. Maria and Leon married at the end of 1948 and were a very devoted couple throughout their marriage.

Maria's family were liberal in their Jewish faith and followed Jewish customs, but attended synagogue only on the High Holy Days. Maria looked back on her childhood years as idyllic. Then the Nazis arrived in Krakow when Operation Barbarossa was initiated by the Germans. They established the ghetto in Krakow in 1941 and the Jewish inhabitants were forced to load their goods onto a cart and move into the ghetto. Maria's family, like the other Jewish families, became more and more impoverished. Her father's business had been confiscated by the Germans previously. Maria's family managed to sustain themselves in the ghetto with the sale of their jewellery and money which had been hidden by Maria's nanny. While living in the ghetto under Nazi occupation, Maria was assigned a job in a German brush factory. She was later given a job working for a German firm which repaired, cleaned and tested guns. Maria described the work as 'not very hard' and it was her task to test the guns after they had been repaired. Her parents did not work, and consequently they were rounded up in the first Aktion, which took place in 1942. The Germans rounded up the Jews, including Maria's parents, who were sent to Belzec where they were murdered. Maria learned this only after the war and after she gave her testimony. Maria recalled her mother's last words to her: 'Don't worry my child, you will live to see better times.' Maria was forced to move in with relatives, because her home was requisitioned for others. The relatives were transported in the second Aktion, and Maria had no choice but to move once again. She was forced to move several times more, but when the ghetto was liquidated at the end of 1942, the prisoners were all forced to march to a camp in Plaszow. They were allowed to take their bedding, which consisted of a pillow, mattress and blanket. Maria was placed in a factory where German uniforms were repaired – they came straight from the front and were often bloodied and dirty. The slave labourers received food which consisted of ersatz coffee, bread and thin soup. Maria witnessed a great deal of violence perpetrated upon the Jewish prisoners in the ghetto and the camp at Plaszow. Shootings, beatings, and torture were daily occurrences.

She had obviously inherited her father's adventurous nature and fearless ability to adapt to changing circumstances. She had the ability to exploit a situation for her benefit, and was quick to seize an opportunity to do so. For example, in Plaszow, when she stood in a queue for selection she made sure that she surreptitiously moved into the survivors' queue with her friend Rutke. There are many other instances reported in her testimony when Maria showed great courage and ingenuity in overcoming the terrible conditions of her internment in Plaszow and elsewhere. She readily agreed to cooperate with the suggestion made by Ada that she steal bullets from the factory in which she worked in Plaszow, and pass them on to be used by the Jewish underground. Later she would steal clothes from the disinfection unit where she worked; Ada agreed to sell them outside the ghetto when her work unit left the camp.

Maria was transferred to a sub-camp where she was given work in an enamel factory which later became a refuge for the workers. The owner, Oskar Schindler, saved the lives of so many of his workers, and treated them sympathetically and humanely. The atmosphere in his factory was very different from other work places.

Plaszow was liquidated in the summer of 1944 and Maria was then transferred to Auschwitz, travelling in cattle wagons. The following day she was moved to Birkenau, where conditions were appalling. The effects of starvation and overwork had already decimated the camp's prisoner population, but in Birkenau they died from the savage treatment meted out to them. Daily Appels were held in the cold and rain, while selections were carried out by a German woman who then sent the prisoners to be tattooed and sent back to Auschwitz. The repeated shuffling back and forth between camps was like an insane dance. Maria was fortunate that she was able to remain together with her friend Rutke throughout their internment. They were a great moral support for one another. Maria was put into a work gang that pointlessly had to cart rocks from one place to another despite their ravaged bodies. Somehow Maria's spirit and determination kept her going, especially after learning that the Red Army was approaching Auschwitz. The Germans, fearful that the Allies would discover the heinous activities that had been carried out in the camp, on 18 March sent the prisoners on a death march to Ravensbruck. The beatings, the shootings, and various other punishments were once again inflicted upon the struggling and starving prisoners. Many collapsed and were immediately shot on the spot. Others simply fell down and died from starvation and disease and despair.

The march lasted for three days, after which the prisoners once again were forced into freight wagons and taken to Ravensbruck, the women's camp. Maria recalled how dogs were set upon them, and many prisoners were severely bitten. On arrival at Ravensbruck the prisoners were taken to a huge, filthy tent where they sat on the ground for one or two weeks, not being given any work, but simply existing. Maria and her friend Rutke volunteered for work and were moved to a camp at Neustadt-Glewe in Germany. From 1 May the Germans began to act more humanely to the captives because they knew that the war was lost. The German guards suddenly disappeared from the camp, and the prisoners wasted no time in raiding the camp storehouse for food and other items. The Americans arrived the following day, to be followed by the Russians. Many of the prisoners became ill from overeating, and many deaths among them were the result of their eagerness to consume as much as possible – their poor malnourished bodies were overwhelmed by the quantity of rich, fatty foods that the Americans gave to the skeletal victims, not understanding that they were unable to digest the largesse.

Maria described in an unforgettable way the scenes that took place when the prisoners realised that they were free to leave the camp. They descended upon the town, where they treated the German inhabitants 'brutally, crudely and heartlessly' (the words used in Maria's testimony). 'A wild feeling of hate, a desire for revenge, wanting to destroy and rob' overtook the freed prisoners.

When the freed prisoners entered the town, the local inhabitants showed their great fear of retribution from the prisoners. Maria depicted how the liberated prisoners rampaged around the town, slaughtering chickens and rabbits for food and treating the Germans as they had been treated. They cooked a piglet which they had come across, ignoring the Jewish prohibition against eating pork. Maria described how she stabbed a man in the stomach when he attempted to stop them from plundering his rabbits. This is told in a matter-of-fact tone without self-consciousness, and without hesitation. Maria's lack of fear and her ability to do whatever was necessary to survive were integral parts of her personality.

Maria had discovered that her immediate family had been murdered by the Germans, and that she was the only survivor except for her grandmother, but she and Rutke were determined to attempt a return to Krakow even if they had to walk all the way. They had to use all their initiative and ingenuity to succeed. They travelled on foot, by horse and cart, by train and by any other means at their disposal. Despite the hardships of their journey, they eventually arrived in Krakow. Somehow Maria had the ability to 'land on her feet', to support herself, which she did by trading in various commodities during the months when she attempted to continue living in Poland while trying to contact relatives living in Australia. She knew that she could not continue to live in Poland. She decided to seek sanctuary with the Australian branch of the family, and even though she did not have their full address she was not deterred. She addressed her letter to WIZO (Women's International Zionist Organization), Sydney, Australia, and, by some miracle, the family found her.

Maria eventually received papers granting her entry into Australia and sailed from Stockholm to Australia in comparative luxury. She sailed on the ship *Sclouidio* to Melbourne, arriving on 30 December 1946.

This was the beginning of a new chapter in Maria's life. She arrived in Melbourne, where she remained for a while, but her restless spirit encouraged her to try Sydney, where she had an aunt who owned a millinery shop. Maria worked for her until she decided to return to Melbourne. There she obtained work in a hat factory and then a knitting factory, following a path taken by many new refugees. During this period, Maria met her future husband, Leon Brooks. Her husband-to-be returned to Melbourne from Shepparton and he and Maria were married on 19 December 1948 in Caulfield, Melbourne. He established a clothing factory in Flinders Lane in Melbourne, the clothing factory colloquially known as being in the 'shmatte' (rag) trade. Later there was the purchase of a grocery store. Maria and Leon had two daughters, Elly and Lorraine, and the two sisters had six children between them:

Michael, Daniel, Joshua, Claire, Eleanor and Matcham, the beloved grandchildren of Leon and Maria. Maria and Leon worked while the children were taken care of by a housekeeper. This did not foster great closeness between the children and their parents, but Lorraine became closer to her father while Elly developed a warmer relationship with her mother.

The parents socialised with other Holocaust survivors and frequently entertained in their home. There were a lot of parties at the home of the Brooks family, and they religiously kept a five o'clock 'happy hour' for their friends. This was one manifestation of Maria's determination to get whatever enjoyment she could out of life. She was determined to 'make up for lost time'. She loved sport, particularly horse-riding and skiing. She was generally determined to get the best out of life, and she indulged her interests without hesitation. She would suddenly decide to go to the ski fields in Mount Buller with friends. She would simply wave goodbye to the family and disappear. She was feisty and always interested in 'how the world functions'. She was independent and very forthright, and even managed to find the time and energy to go back to university. In contrast to this sort of determination, Maria would not discuss the Holocaust with her family. It was not clear whether she wished to spare her children the horror of her experiences, or whether she was unwilling to reinflict the trauma of the Holocaust upon herself. While she was aboard the ship on her way to Australia, Maria started to compile a diary about her life, but no one except her daughter Elly has seen the contents. She has not divulged the contents to anyone. Before she died, she and members of her family visited Poland, where the children and grandchildren learned about the Holocaust and were exposed to some of the realities of what took place during those years.

Maria developed Alzheimer's disease at the age of eighty, and spent the remainder of her life in care. Maria and Leon both died in 2013 and are buried in the Springvale Botanical Cemetery in Melbourne.

THE DESTRUCTION OF JEDWABNE

Rivka Fogel

Jedwabne, a small shtetl twenty-one kilometres from Lodz, had a Jewish population of about 2000 people at the time of the outbreak of the Russian–German war, including 600 Jews from Vizhne, who were brought there at that time. On 22 June 1941, when it became known that the Germans were on their way, every Jewish heart trembled in deathly fear. We remembered well when the area in which we lived was occupied within a short time by the Germans in September 1939. Now we were even more afraid, because on the arrival of the Germans, the Polish hooligans, who had had to behave during the previous two years under Soviet rule, eagerly greeted the Germans. Our fear was soon justified.

Immediately, on the very first day of the German occupation, a whole group of Jews was murdered: the leather-worker Yaakov Katz, the shoemaker Eli Kravietzker, the blacksmith Moshe Weinstein, the trader Moshe Fishman, Chone Goldberg and his son, and many others.

To illustrate the mood of the Jewish population, I will tell you about the following frightful event involving two sisters – one, the wife of Abraham Kovzshansky, and the second, the wife of Shaul Binstein – whose husbands were Soviet activists who had left the town with the

Russian army. The sisters had to suffer invective from the local women because of their husbands, so they took their little children and went to the Sazshelke [river], and there they exchanged their children with one another [probably in order to lessen the horror of their intention to drown themselves and the children], and jumped into the water. Christians happened to notice this and pulled the two women and the children out of the water, but the two women immediately sprang back into the water and drowned.

Jews began to search for ways to save themselves. I do not know what others did, but I and my husband, Yankel Kurtz, and my two sons, Hershele and Leibele, had a discussion with our neighbours, the Pravdes, a couple with two children, and we set off for a little town five kilometres from Jedwabne. We thought that a Christian acquaintance there might help us to hide. However, the Christian was afraid to keep us and sent us to hide in a corn field. The woman, Mrs Pravde, together with her son and mine, left for the town in order to find out what was happening there. However, they never returned to the corn field. We lay in the corn field for a whole day. In the evening, tired and burning from thirst, we went back to our Christian acquaintance in the town. This time he allowed us to lie down on the floor of his little house. We spent the night there.

On the following day, a Christian youth brought us a note from Mrs Pravde: 'My dear ones,' she wrote, 'come home as quickly as possible; my conscience troubles me and I might not survive to see you again'.

While I was reading the note, a Christian suddenly appeared and he yelled at us: 'Run away because peasants from Dor Makovski are on their way here after you.' But it was already too late to run away. The peasants were already at the door. We barely managed to go down to the cellar. But following this, we heard a shout ordering us to emerge from the cellar. First we took out the two children, then I emerged, then when the peasants prepared to shoot into the cellar, the two men also came out.

The few things which we had with us were taken away by the peasants. Our men were told to climb onto a wagon and to leave with them. When they arrived at a small forest they ordered the men to climb down from the wagon and to turn their backs to the peasants. Mr Pravde requested permission to say a confessional prayer before they were killed. The peasants allowed them to do so. Pravde draped a prayer shawl which he had with him over himself and he began to pray. Meanwhile my husband recognised one of the peasants and turned to him saying: 'You know me, you know that we are not communists, do not spill innocent blood, have pity on our wives and children.' It appears that this influenced the peasants. They did not shoot [the men]. What is more, they returned our men to the shtetl.

Meanwhile, one of the local violent criminals, Karolek, was appointed mayor of the town. He chose the worst of the underworld people, who were anti-Semites, as his aides – for example, Kubzhinovski and his son, the brothers Yordanski, and others. They held a series of meetings with the German gendarmes about allowing them to round up in one operation the few remaining Jews. At that time the Germans did not have a system for rounding up Jews, so in the beginning they bargained with the Poles, asking them to find the communists among the Jews. The Poles responded by saying that all Jews were communists. Well, at least leave the tradesmen, the Germans countered, because for the moment we need them. The Poles reassured them that they had their own artisans. It appears that they did not have to use much persuasion with the Germans, who quickly accepted the Polish plan.

SURVIVAL AND SANCTUARY

On 10 July 1941, or fifteen days into the month of Tammuz, the town was surrounded. All Jews were required to leave their homes and to make their way to the market. They were told to bring brooms with them. It was supposed to look as if the Jews were called to sweep the streets. My husband and the two children immediately left. I remained for a while longer at home in order to lock up the house and to take the wheat and seeds grinder which we had been given. I also wanted to go to our neighbours, the Pravdes, to see what they were going to do. Mr Pravde was standing in his dyeing workshop and was busy dyeing a pair of trousers for a policeman. He thought that possibly this might help him. I had not yet managed to say anything when Pravde's wife ran in shouting: 'Chaim Yossel, run away because things are bad.'

I completely lost my senses and instead of going to where my husband and children were, I went together with the Pravdes in the direction of the manor courtyard and we hid in the bushes. I had in mind to jump up and to run back, but the Pravdes held me back with force, and asked me not to go because if I were to emerge, someone might see us.

Suddenly, footsteps were heard very close to us. A Christian passed by. Pravde noticed another one, Yordanski, and immediately after that we heard a shout: 'Help!' followed by a plea not to kill [us], a din with shoving and moaning. Later, we found out that not far from our hiding place a Jewish young man, Josef Levin, was killed. Later we became aware of what had happened to the whole Jewish community at the market.

From eleven o'clock in the morning under a scorching sun the Jews were kept at the market place for the whole day. In groups of forty men the Jews were sent to the cemetery. They were told to dig trenches, into which they were thrown and buried while still alive. Between one bloody action and another, the hooligans joyously entertained themselves with the Jews from the market. They removed Lenin's statue from its pedestal, placed it on a plank and ordered the Jews to carry it while marching and singing Bolshevik songs. They took the old rabbi, Rav Avigdor Bialostotzski, put a heavy stone on his head and led him like this around the whole market. Then they took the daughter of Yudke Nadolnes, Gittele, decapitated her, and played with her head as if it were a ball. Towards evening a person by the name of Vashilevski came to the market and read out to the remaining Jews a death sentence stating they would be burned alive. In his opinion this was a very mild way of dying. He stressed that it was going to be done because all the remaining Jews were decent; otherwise they would die in the same way as those who had been buried alive.

Tins of benzene were standing ready and a command was given to get moving. As we learned later the Jews tried not to go. The hooligans, however, went to the German police who gave them several rifles. All the Jews were chased into Shlishanski's barn which was not far from the cemetery; the walls of the barn were splashed with benzene and set alight. From our hiding place we could hear in the distance horrible screaming which carried through the fields on the side of the cemetery.[1]

Before I continue with further incidents, I want to talk about two occurrences, one of which illustrates how a person can reach the highest form of Kiddush Hashem [to die as a martyr in God's name], and the second – to fall to a base level of cowardice and treachery.

There were two Jews who lived in our shtetl. One was called Israel Grandovski, owner of a wagon and clearly a coarse person. The second was Michal Korapatve, a carpenter, a fine gentleman, a member of the synagogue council and an observant religious Jew. There was an incident with the second Jew in 1939, after the Polish–German battles, when a Polish pilot was hiding at his home. The Poles from the town knew this, and therefore, they wanted to repay Korapatve by saving him and his wife and family from death. They told him to leave the market because he was the only Jew who deserved to live. Korapatve's wife and children stood by with tears in their eyes and waited for their father to go home with them. However, he refused to do so and said: 'I am going wherever the rabbi and the other Jews go.' When one of his daughters saw that her father would not be persuaded, she tore herself from her place, fell upon her father and began kissing him. Weeping, she said to him that she was going with him. They left together and joined all the other Jews on their road to death.

The wife of the first Jew, Israel Grandovski, went to the priest's house, fell at his feet, kissed his hands and begged him to save her and her husband and children from being killed and if he did so, she and her family would convert. This actually happened. Almost the whole Jewish community in the town went away for the sake of 'Kiddush Hashem' and Israel Grandovski and his family went to the church. That same night, after the destruction in our shtetl, we quietly stole away from our hiding place, and by means of various roundabout routes we went back home. We gathered in the Pravdes' stable and remained there for three days. We thought that other than us there were no more Jews in the town. However, later a small group of Jews turned up. From the 2000 people who had made up the Jewish community, there remained only a total of 125 souls.[2]

After this bloodthirsty orgy, the Polish community's hunger to kill subsided somewhat. They insulted us, made us do heavy work, but for the moment they let us live. So, between life and death, we suffered for two months. All of a sudden we received an order to assemble before the magistrate. As no good could come of it, we were not keen to follow the order, and I and the Pravde family decided to escape to Lomzhe.

At that time Lomzhe Jews were enclosed in a ghetto. Conditions there were difficult. There was nothing to eat, no fuel to heat the houses. Endangering our lives, we slipped out to the Aryan side of the ghetto in order to sell something for a little food.

A week after I arrived in the Lomzhe ghetto, a selection took place there, and 2000 Jews who did not have work permits were taken to the Getshin Woods where they were shot. By chance, I stood in the line for pregnant women, and despite neither having a work permit myself nor having a husband with a work permit, on this occasion too I was saved. I lived with the Ostrolenk/Holtzman family, mother and son and four daughters. Also living there was a relation of mine, Chaia Etke Dronzhek, and her two daughters. Altogether ten people lived in two rooms. Suddenly, the oldest Holtzman daughter, Chaia-Freda, found out that the Germans were going to completely liquidate the Lomzhe ghetto. So, she discussed this with a Pole, Pshikadnia, whom she knew and who promised that he would help to save her. In a group we stole out of the ghetto and went to Pshikadnia. But when he saw us, he was shocked and began to shout that he was not prepared for such a large number of people. Despite this, he did not chase us away, but hid us in a cellar where we remained for the whole night. Before daylight, he took us to the Getshin Woods. There we dug a trench in which we hid. Pshikadnia would come to us often with food, and later he even took us out of the ghetto, with the four surviving people who had lived with us, so together we were again ten people.

After remaining in the trench for eight days we saw a peasant with a rifle. We were certain that our end had come. But he did nothing to us, and told us to run away. Again, we left to wander and after several unsuccessful attempts were made to be hidden by Christians,[3] the group of ten people decided to split up, each to go his own way and leave our fate to God's will.

For two years I wandered in the forests until the Russians arrived and saved me. Aside from myself, three daughters of the Holtzman family also survived. Their mother, the oldest sister who saved us from the ghetto, and their only brother, Chaim, were all killed. Chaia Etke Dronzhek and her three-year-old child were also killed. Her thirteen-year-old daughter, Rochele, who stayed with Gentiles disguised as a Christian child, survived. But Rochele's name is now 'unmentionable', the Jewish girl from whom I separated in the forest. She is presently eighteen years of age and is a nun in a Lomzhe convent.

Before I left Poland I went to see her. I wanted to save her from the Jesuits' devious hands, but Rochele did not want to go. She was by then very, very distant from the Jewish people.

More about Rivka Fogel (Rywka Fogiel)

Rivka was born on 1 November 1909 in Rydzewo in Poland. Her parents were Yakow Shlomo Nadborny and Cywi Kac. Rivka married three times. Her first husband was Jakob Kurcz, and he and Rivka had three children, Herzl, Miriam and Leibl; Jakob and their three children perished during the Holocaust. Rivka's second husband was Mosek Fogel, with whom she emigrated from Europe to Australia. Rivka Fogel and Mosek Fogel arrived in Melbourne on 13 November 1947. They sailed to Australia on the ship *Tidewater*. Elias Szydlo was Rivka's third husband. Rivka and Mosek are buried in the Necropolis Springvale in Melbourne.[4] Rivka was ninety years old when she died, and the plaque on her grave mentions her second and third husbands.

In his book *Neighbours: The Destruction of the Jewish Community in Jedwabne, Poland*,[5] historian Jan Gross describes a conversation he had with Rivka Fogel in which she provided him with the details of what occurred in Jedwabne when Poles attacked and killed many Jews. She describes in detail the massacre of the Jewish community in all its horror. She was one of the very few who survived the murder of so many, and was an important witness to the events of that day.

IN THE CAMPS AROUND POSEN

Shlomo Lipman

As soon as the Germans entered our town, a deluge of different edicts poured out daily, making our lives more difficult and horrible. [We had to give them] all sorts of contributions, they took away Jewish assets, even bedding, chased us out of our houses and so on. Then came the calamity of assigning work for us, sending us to labour camps. They, the Judenrat [in the ghetto of Ozorkow], had to provide young, able-bodied people to work for the Germans and they had to pay for the workers' upkeep.

A little later the Germans themselves carried out a 'recruiting drive' for work. This was done in the following way: all men, women and children were chased into a large synagogue, where everyone was ordered to undress completely, and then the Germans organised a sorting process. They stamped everyone's hindquarters just as one stamps horses. The sign 'A' indicated 'capable of work', the letter 'B' meant 'unsuitable for any work'.

At first, we did not attribute any special meaning to the letter 'B' which was an immediate death sentence. We only found this out later. Almost all the able-bodied people were sent to labour camps in the Poznań[1] area. I too was sent away. The remainder, the sick and weak, together with a number of healthy tradesmen, stayed behind in Ozorkow and worked in the local German workshops. This continued until the summer of 1942.

Some time later, the elderly, the sick, women and children, were sent to Chelmno where they were all murdered. The people, naked, were thrust into covered trucks which were driven to the nearest forest and they were all gassed in the trucks on the way. In the forest their bodies were thrown into a mass grave and burned. That was Chelmno; there my wife and child too were murdered.

In Ozorkow only the tradesmen who were confined to a ghetto were left. However, a few months later the Jews of Ozorkow were annihilated. They had been sent to Lodz where they were to share the fate of most of the Jews in Lodz.

The work and the conditions in my camp were extremely difficult. We had to hand over everything that we had with us, money and goods. It was forbidden to buy food. Hunger in the camp was appalling, but to buy something surreptitiously warranted a death sentence. However, there were those who had organised their lives by not giving up all that they had, and by hiding it wherever they could. They also bought food. A few Jews were found out and, as a result, they were then killed.

One Sunday all the Jews from the camps in the area were assembled in the camp stadium. A gallows was erected there, and the Nazi representative of Posen, Gauleiter Greiser, delivered a speech to the Jews. He said something to this effect: 'You Jews have been selected for death. You can prolong your lives only by means of work and more work. We are not afraid to carry out our rules; that is, to hang all of you to the very end when you transgress the rules of National Socialism. Here are the first three who are going to face the consequences for buying a piece of bread for themselves.'[2]

Three Jews were hanged in front of everyone. 'This is only an example to scare you,' Greiser's representative said afterwards. Almost every week, groups of transgressors were caught and openly hanged.

I was incarcerated in this camp for about two years. With the passage of time at least 120 people were killed. Among the condemned there were many courageous people who went heroically to their deaths. I want to mention two of them whose names I remember. One of them was named Fishel Engel from Turek. On the way to be hanged he said to the Gestapo personnel: 'You murderers, you should know that your day of reckoning will come.' And he said to us: 'Be bold until the last moment, and if you should survive, take revenge.' The name of the second one was Mottek Schwartz, a young man from Koil (in Polish, 'Kala'). He called out to us: 'You must live in order to take revenge.'

On one occasion seven people were brought to be hanged. However, the gallows could only take three people at a time. At that time, I worked in a building where there was a tailoring workshop. There was a long corridor there. We suddenly saw how they [the Germans] were chasing seven people into the corridor. One of them begged us for a piece of bread. He was hungry. A second person responded by saying: 'Don't take away the small piece of bread from these people; they are alive and need to eat. Are you afraid that you will faint before going to the gallows?' 'At least I want to be replete before I am hanged,' he begged. Another asked for a cigarette.

Naturally we were ready to give them some bread. But how could we do so when their hands were tied behind their backs? We placed pieces of bread on a board and each of the condemned men bent his head down in order to reach the morsel, just like animals. Three of them were later taken to the gallows and hanged.

A very strange thing happened one day while three Jews were being hanged. The rope for one of them, Lazer Zizovsky from Lodz, tore. Zizovsky fell down to the ground, opened his eyes and looked at his two friends hanging above him. One of the Gestapo men ran to him and placed a second noose around his neck. This time the rope remained whole.

A great many people in the camp died from hunger. Every day a wagon would enter the camp and it would be loaded up with naked corpses, stacked like calves, and taken away to be burned.

In March 1943 the Poznań camps were liquidated. I and my two brothers together with a group of 250 people were sent to Zbaszyn – a town in western Poland on the former Polish–German border. There I worked at earthworks for five months under the guard of Poles. However, after the Warsaw ghetto uprising we were sent to Auschwitz. We travelled for two days. In the middle of the night we arrived at a forest. The train stopped and we were driven out of the wagons. The place was lit up and heavily guarded. SS men chased us to freight trucks which were standing ready for us. Things soon became clear to us: the weak and the sick were sent to their deaths. The healthy ones went into the camp for work. When we arrived in the camp we came across camp inmates of different nationalities. During a conversation with Jewish inmates we were made aware that we were among the lucky ones because part of our transport had been sent straight to the gas chambers.

For eight days we were chased, trained, and learned the 'rules' for camp inmates. During that same period they burned [tattooed] numbers on our arms and then they sent us to work. They arranged us in various work kommandos and each group had to do different jobs: in coal pits, ammunition factories and many other places of work. My brothers and I were sent to work in a coal pit. This, however, was alright because during the few days which we had spent in Auschwitz itself, we suffered terribly, not only from the Germans, but also from criminals and underworld characters who were brought there from all the prisons and they became our bosses. Various Poles, Latvians and other anti-Semites tricked and harassed us.

The difficult work conditions and hunger led to people becoming emaciated and sick in our coal pit; the workers called them 'muselmann'.[3] Twice a week – Mondays and Thursdays – the truck with a red cross on it came from Auschwitz, and those no longer able to work were taken away. Healthy people were brought to replace them, and the exhausted people were taken away to be killed. Fresh workers filled their place. In the terrible conditions in which we lived we devised certain 'preparations', but the Germans somehow got to know about our plans and a number of people were sent to Auschwitz.

A resistance effort was difficult, virtually impossible. Despite this a plan was hatched to carry out a revolt. The belief that one could escape from that place alive was hopeless. Every fifty metres there was an observation tower with a machine gun. The surroundings were always lit up and encircled by electrified barbed wire. In addition the enclosure was fortified and strengthened even more. But without considering the difficulties, we began the secret work of digging an underground tunnel through which to escape. We dug an underground exit with spades and our naked hands. But the plan fell through. A German prisoner by the name of Franz was a kapo in the coal mine, and he betrayed the group. Whoever was caught at the work [of digging the tunnel] was sent to Auschwitz. The leader of the group was hanged on the spot, openly.

One particular day I felt that I could no longer work in the coal pit. I still had a disease, an infirmity, from the second Poznań camp.

The work in the coal pit was very difficult for me, more so as one received fifty lashes for not fulfilling the quota. I decided to approach the camp elder about my sickness during an Appel, telling him that I have an infirmity and cannot work. Two camp elders were present. One of them was known as a better person. His name was SS man Baumgarten. I presented myself to him. He listened to me and asked: 'If that is so, how did you come here? This is no place for those like you,' he said, 'there is no room here, your place is in the "heaven-kommando": that is, the crematorium'. He told me to appear before the camp doctor. The camp doctor there was a prisoner, a Jew from Czechoslovakia – Orlick. One understood that the doctor himself was not trusted with medical examinations. There was always a trustee from the SS men with him. When the doctor had listened to my complaints, he asked me, surprisingly, if I knew what would happen to me. 'Better,' he said, 'bite your lips and continue to work with the last of your strength. Do you not know what such a thing as stopping work "tastes" of?' With a pretence of anger, he seemingly started to shout at me so that the SS man could hear: 'You are lazy, go to your work.' I quickly dressed myself in my rags, went down the steps and hastily went back to work.

However, the doctor remembered me. The next day after lunch he met me and stood still. He told me that I should use all my strength to continue to work. He knew with certainty that I was there with two brothers. The war was almost at an end. This was in 1943 when the Russians reconquered Kharkov and went on to Kiev.

Though I knew that my parents, my wife and child, were no longer alive, the instinct to live was very strong, and the doctor's words gave me added courage. A few weeks later, the same doctor came across a lighter type of work for me in the camp itself, and I returned slowly to a better state of health. Yet, soon after that I was again sent to work in the coal pit. In this manner I worked for the whole of 1944 – a hard, bitter sort of labour in the wet pit where we sometimes had to work lying on our stomachs on the wet soil. On the way from work when I was exhausted, drained, broken with the others, I decided not to return to work and adopted the attitude of 'what will be, will be'. We often received news about the front. Sometimes even a newspaper would be brought to the camp. All our hopes were dependent on the Russian offensive, but it didn't happen. The front was stalled. I remembered that the camp doctor had promised that when he had the opportunity to operate on me, he would do so. I presented myself to him and requested that he should operate on me because I could no longer hold out. The doctor decided to carry out the operation. However, a few days after the operation, the major Russian offensive began. That was in January 1945. When the Russians advanced rapidly our camp started to be evacuated while I was lying in bed, post-operation. Shortly before their arrival I had agreed to have surgery. After the operation the doctor made the first arrangement for me to join the evacuation transport, because everything that remained there would be destroyed. A few hours later, the doctor shared with me that the camp elder had said to him: 'Every weak person who is unable to walk, and lags behind, will be shot en route.' Therefore the doctor persuaded me to remain in bed because I would certainly not be able to cope with the journey. I remained while waiting for a miracle. My brothers went with the transport. They [the Germans] took people from Auschwitz and the surrounding camps and drove them day and night in the direction of Sudetenland. The weak ones of the transport were shot on the way.

The remaining sick people in the nearby camps were 'liquidated' in different ways. Many were shot in their beds; in other camps they were set alight together with the hospital buildings. However, they did not manage to destroy our hospital. The onward march of the Red Army progressed forward rapidly. The chaos was so great that it was fairly easy to overlook something and to leave it intact. This is what happened to our hospital building. We were saved from death by chance.

On 25 January 1945, the Russians arrived at our camp and liberated us. The severely ill were immediately transferred to Krakow, but we were kept in the same place and received the finest help and nutrition. As soon as one could stand up, we went on our way to find our former homes. I went to Lodz and afterwards to Ozorkow; there were no members of my family there, and I did not meet any acquaintances from home, so it was back to Lodz. There I came across one of our prisoners, Solomanchik. I asked him if he knew the fate of my brothers. He told me that my brothers had died during an air raid. The older brother was taken to a camp further away. One day he did not go to work but remained in the camp. The camp elder, Franz, who was with them, went to him and called out: 'There is no such thing as wandering around the camp and not working.' He took my brother to a log, directed him to put his head on the log and decapitated him.

Later, when the Russians occupied the camp where Franz was in charge, the surviving Jewish prisoners had the 'honour' of taking revenge on him. They themselves hanged him.

Solomanchik gave me a leather band which he had taken off my dead brother and told me about the exact place where my brother was buried.

More about Shlomo Lipman and Ester Lipman, second wife of Shlomo

Shlomo (originally Zlamek) Lipman was born on 18 February 1907. He lived in Ozorkow until the Germans arrived. Shlomo's first wife and child were murdered in Chelmno by the Germans. In 1946, after liberation, Shlomo married his cousin Ester in Lodz, where they spent some time. Loneliness and the desire to re-establish a family led to many survivors entering marriage, sometimes to people they had known for a short time only. Shlomo, however, married a family member who had also lived in Ozorkow and they were acquainted through the family.

In her testimony, which she gave later at the Melbourne Holocaust Centre, Ester described how her family lived before the Germans invaded Poland in 1939. Her father had a menswear clothing business and Ester knew how to run the business. Her knowledge was to stand them in good stead when they later settled in Australia, where Shlomo and Ester opened a menswear clothing shop. In Ozorkow, she had lived with her parents and siblings in a small flat, and the family was very close. Religion was very important to her parents, who were always aware of their duty as Jews to practise charity. Sadly, Ester's parents and siblings, four brothers and two sisters, were murdered by the Germans in the gas chambers of Auschwitz.

The Germans arrived in Ozorkow in 1939, where they quickly established a ghetto at the end of 1939. There Ester was witness to many atrocities committed by the Germans. On one occasion, as a lesson, the ghetto inhabitants were forced to watch the hanging of ten men who were guilty of minor infringements. Ester described the Jewish police as corrupt and brutal, and was loath to speak about them while giving her testimony. The Jews were rounded up and chased into a stadium where they were forced to undress completely, thus humiliating them. The children were removed in trucks, and the men sent to work as slave labourers. Ester and a number of other women were returned to the ghetto, where they had to work making women's clothing for the Germans, who sent the clothes back to Germany for use by the German citizens. After the Ozorkow ghetto was liquidated in 1940, Ester was sent to the Lodz ghetto, where she lived until 1943. This period ended when Ester was transported to Auschwitz and then to Bergen-Belsen. She had a short stay in each of these camps and was then transferred to Salzwedel women's camp in Germany. The places in which she survived under German rule and after liberation were: 1939–1940 Ozorkow ghetto, Poland; 1940–1943 Lodz ghetto, Poland; 1943 Auschwitz, Poland; 1943–1945 Bergen-Belsen, Germany; 1943–1945 Salzwedel camp, Germany; 1945–1946 Lodz, Poland; 1946 Landsberg Displaced Persons camp, Germany; and 1946–1947 France.

After she was liberated by the Americans, she returned to Lodz, and she and Shlomo attempted to remain in Poland, but the frequent pogroms which took place against surviving Jews whose homes had been in Poland before the German invasion and the devastation of the Jewish population meant that it was too intimidating for the couple to live in such a dangerous and hate-filled atmosphere. They paid a guide to take them across the border to Germany, where they successfully sought out the Landsberg Displaced Persons camp.

From the Landsberg Displaced Persons camp they applied for Australian visas, which they eventually obtained with the help of a rabbi in Australia, who sent them the required permits. They travelled to Paris by train, where they hoped to embark on a ship to Australia. During the period in Paris, while they were waiting for their Australian visas, they were helped by the Joint, who located Ester's cousin and arranged for Shlomo and Ester to be accommodated with the family. Meanwhile Shlomo and Ester worked in a clothing factory, so they were able to reimburse their cousin for taking care of their needs.

In 1946 when their necessary papers had arrived, they embarked on a ship which previously had carried troops to their destination. Shlomo and Ester sailed from Marseilles on the *Johan de Witt* and arrived in Sydney on 16 March 1947. They then travelled from Sydney to Melbourne.

They settled in Melbourne and eventually established a clothing factory of their own. Their business was very successful, which enabled them to be able to return to Paris in order to visit their family again. They made it their mission to share their success with survivor friends, and were extremely grateful that Australia had opened its doors to them and given them the opportunity to live full lives. Previously known as Zlamek, Shlomo changed his first name because he thought 'Shlomo' was more suitable to life in an English-speaking country.

In Melbourne Ester bore a son.[4] The baby was born with a severe congenital condition, which later confined him to a wheelchair. Their son's illness weighed heavily upon Ester and Shlomo but they devoted themselves to his care for the whole of his life. He was a wheelchair user for the remainder of his life and became a successful commercial artist. In one instance, he applied for permission from Warner Brothers in America to paint various Disney characters on the walls of children's wards in the hospital in which he had spent some time. Hospital personnel were delighted with the results of his work. Sadly, he died at the age of thirty-five.

While Ester and Shlomo were content in Melbourne, they felt that Sydney might offer greater opportunities for financial success, so they moved to Sydney, but often visited Melbourne and the friends they had there: Melbourne held many happy memories for them. After settling in Sydney, where they remained, they had two more children: a son, Les, and a daughter, Ruth.

At home, the family lived a traditional Jewish life, the Shabbat table groaning with an abundance of food. This was concrete evidence of their success, of which they were very proud. Sadly, though, Shlomo lost his faith after experiencing the torture of the camps and seeing people live and die so horribly. He could not conceive of the religious Jews, especially the rabbis, maintaining their belief in a just God. Despite this, Jewish tradition was still maintained in their lives, and Shlomo and Ester found comfort in the familiar rituals which reinforced their Jewishness. And despite their problems, Shlomo still displayed a fine sense of humour, often expressed in a particularly Jewish way.

Shlomo and Ester mixed socially with other Holocaust survivors. Their daughter Ruth described how, during her early years, she assumed that all adults had numbers tattooed on their arms. Neither Shlomo nor Ester would talk to their children about their experiences during the Holocaust. If Ruth walked into a room while they were having a discussion about the Holocaust, they would stop talking or would change the subject. While they did share their past with other survivors, they were very secretive with their immediate family.

Shlomo loved Australia (proudly becoming a citizen in 1955) and was always grateful for the lifestyle that he and Ester were able to maintain. However, even though their existence seemed, on the surface, to be fulfilling, even joyful, both he and Ester were highly traumatised by the terrible events they had experienced during the Holocaust. Shlomo suffered from hideous nightmares and was awoken by his own screams almost nightly. His first family, who perished during the Holocaust, was out of bounds for family discussion. He and Ester forbade their children from asking questions: indeed, Ruth describe it as "forbidden territory". And when Ester was hospitalised during her senior years, she was reluctant to have X-rays carried out because, as she told Ruth in Yiddish, there were faces communicating with her that wanted to take her to the gas chambers.

Although Ruth felt loved by her parents, Shlomo and Ester found it difficult to display their feelings, or to be demonstrative towards her. It was as though they were afraid to invest too much emotion in the family for fear they might once again suffer the devastating loss of a loved one. This situation was very painful for Ruth, who felt the lack of openly expressed love from her mother and father. She said that Shlomo and Ester often seemed 'frozen in time'. Trust was difficult for them.

Ruth described her family life as 'austere', because both her parents were so traumatised from their war experiences and, in addition, her disabled brother required very demanding care, needing much compassion and understanding. Shlomo and Ester were over-protective of Ruth, and she led a heavily controlled existence. Very strict guidelines dominated her life, from controls on her privacy to whom she associated with. Her behaviour was constantly supervised and monitored. She often felt guilty when she wanted more personal freedom, feeling that it was wrong of her to want something against her parents' wishes. Guilt often stopped her from following her own instincts because she feared causing Shlomo and Ester greater suffering than they had already experienced from the trauma of the war years.

As an adult, Ruth married Gary Eckstein and they had two daughters, Donna and Lisa, granddaughters for Shlomo and Ester.

Shlomo's greatest joy was teaching his offspring to speak Yiddish, imparting to them his love of the language. He loved Jewish art and was very much involved in expressions of Jewish culture. He also found satisfaction in being an active participant in the Yiddish Folk Centre, where he found cultural fulfilment in the discussions and other activities that took place there. He and Ester were also enthusiastic supporters of the Sydney Jewish Museum, and they set up a Memorial Endowment Fund in their name.

Throughout their lives, they refused to buy German products or to speak Polish, which they associated with their memories of Polish collaboration with the Germans.

Shlomo died on 6 March 1980, aged seventy-three. Ester passed away in 2006, but before her death she expressed her opinion that she was physically greatly affected by her Holocaust experiences, and complained that her eyesight suffered markedly. Shlomo and Ester are buried together.

Ruth has transmitted to her own children the facts of the Holocaust and her parents' experiences. She feels that it is necessary to pass on the truth so that it is never forgotten. For this reason, she believes in suitable memorials in remembrance of the Holocaust, and Holocaust education for school children. She herself has no desire to visit Poland, but would allow her children to do so. Ruth fears greatly a recurrence of the Holocaust; she keeps abreast of current world affairs, seeking reassurance.

ONCE UPON A TIME THERE WAS A SHTETL, BENDZIN

David Tuszynski

There was once a shtetl of Jewish tailors – Bendzin. From very early until late at night, the music of Singer sewing machines could be heard. It was the music of hard work, of bitter need, of a hard life, but also that of boisterous youth, political party intellectuals, pious Jews, Chassidic Jews who lived, who strove in the small Jewish shtetl, Bendzin.

The Hitler hydra extinguished that life forever, transformed it into ash. There remained only a few Jews from the tailor-town, Bendzin, saved by a miracle and dispersed all over the world, a few witnesses of German bestiality.

May these words, inadequate in print, written not in ink, but in blood, be a modest contribution to the monument of my birthplace, Bendzin.

* * *

Bendzin was one of the oldest and most liked Yiddish settlements in Poland. When that community was founded it bore the name of Krakowek. At the time, the settlement stretched from the Strikover highway past the Jewish cemetery to the hills. The Polish Duchess, Anna Lasotski, brought the first weavers into that settlement. Consequently the community developed and began to extend its boundaries. The town took on the name of Bendzin.

Jewish tailors from various places began to migrate to Bendzin and within several generations a local tailoring industry [i.e. a cottage industry] developed, for which the shtetl became known very widely. The cottage industry marked life in the shtetl. By 1772 Bendzin was already famous for its huge tailoring industry. Until 1914, the great Czarist Russia was flooded with inexpensive products from the Bendzin tailors. In the years between the two world wars, the goods from Bendzin were exported to a great number of countries in Europe as well as countries in other parts of the world. An important role was played by the Jewish wholesale exporters such as Frankenstein, Tushinski, Solkovitz and others.

In 1939 when war broke out, the Bendzin population numbered 17,000, among them 9000 Jews, almost all of them tailors.

The Bendzin Jews not only worked, they also took a lively interest in social politics and the cultural life of the shtetl, and they had their representatives in the town council, and in court; they had religious and secular education, and cultural societies. The Jews had a life of material poverty, but a spiritually rich one, as well as socially and culturally.[1]

* * *

September 1939.

The Germans are on the march. Mobilisation and tumult. In Eastern Poland thousands of Jews are frantically running away. Jewish masses pass through Bendzin en route to Warsaw. The Jews of Bendzin leave their new machines; they go out in the streets in order to give help to the passing Jews. They share food, they give medicinal aid and they provide beds for those who are stopping for a day or two in the shtetl.

On Wednesday, the sixth day of war, Bendzin was bombed. Fire and smoke envelop the town. The streets – Saint Anna Street, a portion of Pilsodski Street and Rogovski Street – disappear in the smoke. At this time many local residents and refugees from Lodz, Kalisz and other towns were killed.

A few days later the Germans occupied our town and a series of events began: searches and robbery, kidnapping for work, insults, humiliation, beatings and torture. A large group of 'intelligentsia', and various community leaders, were arrested and sent away. They never returned and to this day no one knows where they went.

On Yom Kippur,[2] the day after the Germans burned down the synagogue, they led old rabbi Bornstein outside into the street and set his beard alight. Chasing him, beating him, they took him, exhausted and confused, to the train station and sent him to Krakow. A few days later, broken and sick, he was returned to Bendzin in order to send him together with the other aged people to the gas chambers [at Auschwitz].

Kidnappings for work took place every day. A number of the people who were taken were sent to the back of the town on the road to Galkowek, where people were tortured and then buried alive.

In the second half of December 1939, the SS man Kaufman came to Bendzin and a few days later the first transport began. Jews were collected from a whole row of streets to be sent away. Most significant for us were pronouncements made by the Jews Zagan and Kleinbaum stating that the local Jews, tailors by trade, could be used for work for the army, and the main thing – with the help of a huge sum of bribery money in cash and in gold [handed to the Germans] – was that the transports were stopped. Factories were subsequently established in Bendzin for the German military.

In the first few months of 1940, a ghetto was organised in Bendzin. The Judenrat was created with Ika Fishke, Police Kommandant Perlmutter, known by the name of 'Enthusiastic guzzler' [spry drunkard] as the leader. As if the Germans were not enough, we also had to put up with inordinate trouble from the local Jewish 'authorities'.

Despite hunger, cold and repressive measures in the ghetto, the work in the tailoring factories went on. We completed clothes for the Germans. From time to time German 'guests' would come to Bendzin. Especially well known were the SS men Fooks, Richter and Shvinto. Those particular names caused fear and horror among the Jewish population in the Bendzin ghetto. Through various ways and means, they looted the last of the possessions of the Jewish population – gold, jewellery and furs. They would get drunk and the Judenrat then had to provide them with alcohol: wine, liquor and cognac. They wanted women and the Judenrat had to supply women for them. The 'chairman' Fishke obediently followed orders, carried out everything that they demanded of him.

Nevertheless, one could say that life in the ghetto in 1940 proceeded as 'normal'; somehow we lived. Later, the situation became much worse, incomparably so. Already in the first few days of January 1941, an order was issued for ten Jews to be offered up to be hanged publicly. A gallows was erected at the site of the burned synagogue; the Judenrat, according to the order, had to provide the ten Jews to be hanged. And the Judenrat carried out the order. The whole Jewish population from the ghetto were brought to the execution and they were forced to watch this piece of 'work'. At noon, the ten Jews, with their hands tied behind their backs, were brought to the gallows. Among the victims there was a pious, sick woman, Mondzia, and among them was another woman, Fayge 'Watercarrier'. The rest were men, among whom there was Yudel 'Watercarrier', Orbach, Hoizer and others. Hoizer went to the gallows with a shout: 'We are going to our death as martyrs [kiddush hashem, the sanctification of God's name], take revenge!' Yudel 'Watercarrier' called out: 'Until now I was a simple water carrier, tomorrow I will be among the holy ones [the kiddushim].'

After this incident, it was quiet for a few weeks, but later it all started again.

An order was issued that all the old and sick were to come to be tattooed. All the old people were then assembled in Badaver's house, men and women. They all had to undress completely. From the outset, the SS men had organised entertainment for themselves. The naked old men and women had to dance and illustrate various acts which simply cannot be described. They compelled the Jews to act out different scenes, and beat them on their naked bodies and heads. Afterwards, when the SS personnel had had enough of the 'performance', they came to 'stamp' all those present. The tattoos were engraved on the sex organs.

Those who were able and had received the 'stamp' with the letter 'B' turned to go home. The remainder were sent away to their deaths.

On 15 and 16 May 1942, a group of SS men together with Biebow as chief arrived in the Bendzin ghetto. Biebow's reputation already preceded him. His name evoked a terrible fear in everyone. Biebow gave an order that the mothers had to bring to him their children aged twelve or younger. That day it rained in Bendzin, it poured, and yet, in the streets of the ghetto, combed, neatly dressed Jewish children were led by their mothers. The mothers cried and the children comforted them as they attempted to placate them with words something like, 'Mama don't cry, why are you crying?'

All the children were brought to the magistrates' building where they remained with their mothers for the whole day. Night fell, tired children fell asleep on the floor beside their mothers. Some children cried, and others asked: 'Mama, let's go home, why do we not go home? Why is it so dark? Why are the lights not switched on?'

Suddenly, at three o'clock in the morning, the hall became light. A noise, a drunken shout, woke the children. An order was heard: 'Give up all the children,' and after that, the children were torn away from their mothers. Weeping from mothers and children, a shout, pleading and the SS men snatch the children away from their mothers' wrinkled hands. Children scream and cry: 'Mama, I want to go to you, mama.' The mothers fall to the feet of the SS men, kiss their filthy boots and plead. The SS boots kick heads, shove, wicked laughter resounds through the hall, mixed with the whistle of whips on the bodies of the weeping mothers. The mothers beg: take us with them also, we want to go together with our children. It does not help. The children are taken away, and the beaten, suffering and weeping mothers are left in the hall. One of the Gestapo men, Zeifertt, shouts out: 'The mothers must "kick the bucket" [die] here,' and goes out. From outside children's cries and weeping are heard. After a few minutes it becomes totally silent. At dawn, SS men come in to the mothers and with shouts and beatings they chase the mothers into the street. On the following day the ghetto in Bendzin is emptied of children. Only one mother remained in the ghetto with her child: this was Mira Rozen.

The Judenrat risked itself for her, and the Germans were so 'generous' that they gave a gift, the life of one Jewish child.

The mothers approached the chairman of the Judenrat with the question: 'What about our children? Where were our children sent?' The chairman replied: 'The children are in Lodz, with Rumkowski in Marysin; they are in a children's home there. You will soon see them again.'

After a few days, just as they had taken the children away from Bendzin, so they began to take away the adults. The liquidation of Bendzin ghetto began. People were grabbed from their homes and the factories, and were transported to their deaths. A short time later, the Bendzin ghetto was liquidated. Bendzin became 'Judenfrei' [free of Jews].

More about David (Devi) Tuszynski

Although David was not one of the Jewish survivors who arrived in Melbourne before 1949, the YIVO Committee, which collected and published the seven testimonies that appear in this book, did include David's work in this collection during the period he lived in Melbourne together with his wife. It is not clear when they might have recorded the work, or why they decided to add it to those of the Melbourne survivors. David's two brothers were among the refugees who arrived in Melbourne where they remained and where they were buried. They were Felix (who, like David, was an artist) and Rachmil. Both of these brothers are buried in Springvale Botanical Cemetery. David lived in Melbourne for a period, and then visited Melbourne several times, but always returned to Paris.

The life of David Tuszynski was described by Marcia Feldman as a 'complex collage'.[3] He was born in 1915 in Bendzin, Poland. At the age of six he was already fascinated by drawing, and his maternal grandfather encouraged his interest, even going so far as to buy David pencil and paper for his own use. This was most unusual among the religious families, most of them poor, in the small town of Bendzin. David became an avid reader from early childhood onwards and remained so all his life. Although he became known worldwide as a great master of the art of painting miniatures, he was also inspired to write poetry, which received great acclaim.

His family moved from Bendzin to Plotz (near Lodz), where he lived for twenty years. He studied in Lodz under the direction of Professor Dobrovolski. In 1939 he was mobilised into the Polish army and took part in the defence of Warsaw. The occupation of Poland by the Germans led to his incarceration in a number of concentration camps together with his family. The loss of his parents and brothers affected him greatly and his poetry reflects his anguish. However, he infused his work with images of beauty in contrast to the horrors of the Holocaust.

After the war, David, or Devi, as he was now known, left for Paris, where he became a renowned miniaturist. There he became friendly with celebrated figures like the artist Marc Chagall, Jan Peerce, Marcel Marceau and Charlie Chaplin among others. Devi flourished in Paris and he exhibited widely. His miniatures hang in museums in many different countries in the world including Australia, Monaco, Belgium, Holland and Israel. His work was inspired by the Jewish world before the Holocaust and reflects images of his village, the sights and sounds with which he grew up, religious artefacts and scrolls relating to the Torah and other holy books. His miniatures are drawn in fine detail, and they celebrate life despite the Holocaust. They are suffused with images of flowers, birds and mythical beasts. He describes his contrasting imagery with the words 'the more light there is, the more leaves there grow on the tree and the more shade the tree casts; but the deeper the shade under the tree, the brighter the light in the leaves'.

His grandmother, Felicja Solinski, also lived in Melbourne during the period that Devi and his wife made their home there. She was a great admirer of the couple, and described David in glowing terms in an article dated 25 October 1969:

> I was greatly taken by the simplicity and the unassuming manner in which Tuszynski narrated his experiences, stories and observations. Despite difficult times, harsh conditions, hunger and the ever-present lack of prospects for the future of which he spoke, he never gave up and never lost hope. His stories were of friends: famous writers and artists whom he loved, admired and with whom he shared moments of triumph and sadness. Riveted by his revelations and sincerity, I was transported into a soul-enriching world, and came to understand why he made Paris his second home.

In addition she described him as a man unique in his talents and internationally acclaimed. 'How proud we are he is one of our own! Looking at his hands I saw a path to his heart opening a richness of feeling, boundless imagination and a formidable will. I saw a disciplined work of precision allowing his most original and unusual symbols to reflect a world of emotion and beauty.'

One of Devi's works hangs in the National Gallery of Victoria. The National Archives of Australia have in their collection a film about him. He returned to Paris in December 1962. There he died in 2002 and was mourned by his many friends and admirers.

THE DESTRUCTION OF ZOLOCHIV

Mark Fromer

Three days after the Germans occupied Zolochiv,[1] on 3 July 1941, the Germans, with the help of the local Ukrainian population, organised a pogrom. The local Polish population joined them in beating and murdering Jews. The Jews were beaten with sticks and stones, then shot – on that day 3000 Jewish souls were murdered.

After that bloody pogrom it was quiet for a time. A Judenrat, which was later used as a tool by the Germans to work specifically against the Jews, was formed, in keeping with an order from the German officials. One of the officials from the Judenrat had to allot different types of work to Jews. The Judenrat also carried out various requisitions from the Jewish population. Those who carried out orders from the Judenrat were Jewish policemen who had been appointed to do so. Every Jew who was older than fourteen had to be placed somewhere for work.

Already, during the first weeks of the German occupation of Zolochiv, Jews were expelled from the better areas of the city. In addition, the Jews had to make a contribution [to the Germans].

The Germans prepared at least four slave labour camps for the Jews: Latski, Kozaki, Plukhov and Yakhterov. Notwithstanding that the Judenrat was busy locating people for specific types of work for the

Germans, they [the Germans] started hunting the Jews in the town. Arrests occurred almost daily. Suddenly the Germans, together with the Ukrainian military, closed off the Jewish streets, caught Jews in the streets and in their houses and sent them to different German labour camps. Conditions in the work places were appalling. Every Jew's life depended on the mood and whim of the SS men. Thousands died from starvation, sickness and shooting. It was very difficult to escape from the camp. Victims were hanged for any attempt to escape.

In mid July 1942, news came from Lemberg [Lviv/Lvov] that so-called Aktions were taking place there during which large transports of Jews were being sent from the town to unknown destinations. At the beginning it was thought that they were sending the Jews out to work. It later became apparent that Jews were being sent to their deaths.

Soon enough the Zolochiv Jews were to have a taste of those Aktions. At the end of August 1942, the deportations of the Jews in Zolochiv began. During those deportations, the Germans were helped by Jewish representatives who worked with the Gestapo [in the hope of saving their own lives] and also the Jewish police and officials of the Judenrat.

The transports of the Zolochiv Jews took place on 28 and 29 August. All the Jews were brought to the Judenrat building where selections took place. During those selections 1500 Jews were transported. Selections took place again on 2 and 3 October 1942.

In November, a ghetto was established in Zolochiv; 5000 Jews were concentrated in a small area in the centre of the town, and were surrounded by barbed wire and guarded by Ukrainian guards. At a later period, Jews from the surrounding towns of Sasov, Biali, Kamien and Aleska were brought to Zolochiv. In addition there were camps in Sasov, Yokhi, Latski and Kozaki where several hundred people were incarcerated.

THE DESTRUCTION OF ZOLOCHIV

The ghetto in Zolochiv existed until 2 April 1943. On that day, all the Jews from the Zolochiv ghetto were assembled: they were robbed of everything that they had with them, clothes and other possessions, and thereafter everyone was sent in freight trucks several kilometres behind the town into a forest where all were murdered.

Not far from the village Yelekhovitze, the remainder of the Zolochiv community was killed. Christians who drove the trucks taking the Jews to their execution gave the following detailed information about the slaughter.

> Everyone had to undress completely and stand in a row alongside the pre-prepared trenches. Then the Jews standing on the edges of the trenches were shot. After the murderous task, the graves were filled in [covered with soil]. There were many wounded people who were still alive, however, and they were buried together with the dead. This mass slaughter went on all day. The goods belonging to the victims were subsequently loaded onto the trucks which then left.

A few Jews, who were hidden in their bunkers, remained in Zolochiv after the liquidation of the ghetto. Slowly they were discovered, and within the period of a few weeks, every Thursday and Friday, they were sent in groups to the village, Yelekhovitze, to be executed. After four weeks of searching, the Zolochiv ghetto was cleared of Jews.

During the final liquidation the Germans did not spare the Judenrat and the Jewish police: they too were murdered. Only a few Jews remained in the Zolochiv labour camp, but on 22 July 1943, the labour camp too was liquidated. A portion were sent to do slave labour in Yanover camp behind Lemberg, and the rest, who were no longer able to do any work, were shot. During the same period the camps of Sasov, Plutov, Latski and Kozaki were also liquidated.

The following occurred in the Sasov camp: when the camp was surrounded in preparation for its liquidation, the Jews escaped into the nearby forest. The Germans and the Ukrainians opened fire on the escapees. Hundreds of Jews fell dead, but 150 were successful in escaping and remaining alive. They all hid in the forests. A few hundred Zolochiv Jews as well as Jews from other places had also hidden in the same forests. They remained there until liberation.

Afterwards, as the Soviets arrived in Zolochiv, 150 Zolochiv Jews returned to the town from the forests. This number was all that remained of a community which, in 1941, had numbered 10,000 people.

More about Mark (Mordechai) Fromer

Mark Fromer (also known as Marcus Fromer) was the son of Moses Fromer and Anna Helbraun. In 1927 he was born in the town of Zolochiv, where he was also raised. Zolochiv, in present-day Ukraine, was located in the Tarnopol Voivodeship during the period of the Second Polish Republic from 1923 until 1939. From July 1941 the town was occupied by the Germans, who invaded Poland at the beginning of World War II. They then incorporated it into the General Government, which the Germans had set up in the district of Galicia.

The Fromer family lived a strictly Orthodox Jewish life and managed to survive the war by hiding in a secret bunker. The extended Fromer family all hid together in the bunker for a whole year. They were secretly kept alive by a Polish peasant who received payment from an uncle of Mark Fromer in return for supplying them with food and other necessities. He was the only member of the family who had the financial means to do so, thus saving the lives of the family while they were in hiding in the bunker.

Remarkably, the Fromer family managed to survive the Holocaust without being incarcerated in a ghetto or being sent to a concentration or labour camp. With the exception of the brothers and sisters of Mark Fromer's father, who were all murdered at the hands of the Nazis, the remainder of the family successfully remained in hiding until the end of the war.

In 1949, Mark emigrated to Melbourne. He was sponsored by a cousin in accordance with the requirements of the Australian Government. Life was not easy for the new arrivals, and in 1951 he decided to try life in Israel. However, this was during a period of austerity in Israel, and, after six months of struggling to make a living, he found it even more difficult to make ends meet in the fledgling state than it had been in Australia. Once again, it was time for the family to pack its bags, this time to return to Melbourne.

In Melbourne, the suburb of Carlton had become home to many Holocaust survivors whose mother tongue was Yiddish. The Fromer family joined their fellow countrymen in an area where they could feel at home and where they could reconstruct a life as close as possible to the life they had lived in Eastern Europe. Naturally, there were many adjustments to make in order to integrate into Australian life and still uphold the linguistic and religious life of the Orthodox community.

Later, Mark moved to the suburb of Elwood, where he met Erica Heino, a Pressburg-born Czechoslovakian Holocaust survivor. Mark, who was a very religious man, married her at Adass in East St Kilda in 1961 when he was twenty-nine years old. Erica was then twenty years old.

After settling in Elwood, the Fromer family seem to have been able to put down roots, as they became an integral part of the Elwood Talmud Torah Hebrew Congregation.

Mark initially worked at producing knitwear; however, Chinese imports of knitwear negatively affected the viability of the local manufacture of such goods, so later he established a printing business with the encouragement of his wife, who was a great support to him.

Mark's parents, Moses and Anna [also known as Erica] Fromer, are both buried in Adass Israel Cemetery in Springvale. Mark passed away on 6 April 2007 and is also buried in the Adass cemetery.

ADDENDUM

NOTES PERTAINING TO THE TESTIMONIES

Polish Jews serving in the Polish army

During the 1000 years of the Jewish presence in Poland, Jews served in the Polish army and also participated in all aspects of the Polish economy. They took part in many wars and battles in which Poland fought to defend her independence, fighting against various would-be conquerors such as Austria and Russia. Polish Jews were loyal to the Polish Government and willingly contributed their knowledge and experience to Poland for the good of Polish society. Many Jewish soldiers fought with the Polish army when Poland was struggling against the Soviet Union to maintain her independence between 1919 and 1921. In December 1929, on the initiative of former members of the Polish Legion and members of the Polish Military Organisation, Jews established the Association of Jewish Fighters for Polish Independence. Many of the Jewish fighters achieved the rank of officers in the Polish army.

The Germans invaded Poland at the start of September 1939. The Polish army was totally unprepared for the highly mechanised German forces, which defeated Poland in a matter of days. This was the start of World War II.

From 1939 to 1945, during the time of the German occupation of most of Europe (twenty-one countries), Jews were active participants in Polish underground and partisan movements. Some Polish partisans refused to accept Jews in their 'otriads' (units) so the Jewish partisans fought in all-Jewish units, or together with those Polish partisans who accepted the Jews as comrades-in-arms. Jewish partisans proved to be very skilled in battle. They also took part in the war as members of the Free Polish Army. Klieger notes that some 100,000 Jewish soldiers and officers fought in the battles following the German invasion, which lasted for seventeen days, and he also notes that nearly 20,000 Jews served in the ranks of the Free Polish Army.[1] Thousands of Jews were killed in battle and tens of thousands were taken prisoner by the Germans, as were their Polish comrades. According to the Geneva Convention, approximately 50,000 Jewish soldiers became prisoners of war and were sent to various German concentration camps.[2] Treatment of the prisoners of war varied considerably, depending on the Kommandant of the camp and the German personnel. According to extant Polish documents, the percentage of Jews serving in the Polish army in World War II – when the Germans invaded Poland on 1 September 1939, and in the ranks of the Free Polish Army organised in the Soviet Union and England – was 10 per cent.

The Germans invaded Poland from the west, north and south. Only sixteen days later, Soviet forces invaded Poland from the east, following a secret protocol contained in the Molotov–Ribbentrop pact[3] between the Germans and the Russians. The result was the division of Poland – Russia annexed the entire territory of the Second Polish Republic, while Germany occupied the remainder of the country.

Soviet forces occupied eastern Poland until the summer of 1941, when they were driven out by the Germans in the course of Operation

Barbarossa. The Germans occupied the area until it was re-conquered by the Soviets in the summer of 1944.

Jewish ghettos in German-occupied Europe

In the twenty-one countries occupied by Nazi Germany during World War II, Jews were isolated in ghettos and incarcerated in forced labour, work and transit camps, in addition, of course, to concentration and death camps. Over 42,000 camps and other places of incarceration have been identified.[4] The isolation of the Jews in ghettos, subjecting them to humiliation and discrimination, was the penultimate step to the 'Final Solution' – the extermination of European Jewry.

In September 1939, Reinhard Heydrich, Chief of the German Security Police, issued an order to all the 'Einsatzgruppen' (special detachments) of the Security Police to establish 'cities of concentration' in occupied Polish territory so that Jews could be assembled in one area of each city. In addition, he stated that the areas in which the Jews would be located should be near a railway line. This clearly implied that in the future Jews would be transported by rail to various destinations. He also stated that Jews living in the ghetto would not be allowed outside the ghetto perimeter. Thus he created a method by which Jews could be contained in a closed space, which enabled the Germans to have complete control over their lives. This included the distribution of food supplies, control over working conditions, health and sanitary provisions, habitation, education – in short, all aspects of daily life.

The pretext offered by the Germans for their occupation of Europe and the spread of German power was that they needed 'Lebensraum' (living room), an enlarged country for the further development of their citizens and their economy. Hitler then formulated the following three tenets for the conquest of Lebensraum:

- Space must be sought in Europe only.
- The space must be an area contiguous to the German Reich.
- The resistance of the owners must be broken.[5]

Nazi propaganda minister Joseph Goebbels stated that the Jews must be isolated completely in order to prevent their so-called evil from contaminating the Germans. In Eastern Europe ghettoisation was carried out over the whole territory. Jews from other areas, such as Austria, among others, were brought to Poland. The German propagandists[6] justified the isolation of Jews in ghettos on the basis that they were disease carriers, filthy in their personal habits, professional criminals and black marketeers, rapists of Aryan women and naturally evil. Ian Kershaw states that 'Hitler's mission was to remove Germany's Jewish cancer and to [remove] Germany's Jewish poison.'[7] The Nazis deliberately made conditions in the ghettos incapable of supporting life.

Lodz ghetto, which features in Tobcia Blicblau's testimony, was one of the earliest ghettos to be established by the Germans in occupied Poland. As early as December 1939 plans for the ghetto were drawn up and designated for the Jewish population of the city of Lodz (the second largest city in Poland). The description of the Lodz ghetto stands as an example of how the ghettos were generally run. There were differences between the ghettos arising from the orders given by the kommandant and his staff, but Lodz ghetto illustrates the ethos that prevailed in most of the ghettos. During the German occupation of Lodz, intimidation, round-ups and torture became a reality for the residents. They were also deprived of making a living as all Jewish businesses were confiscated, and Jewish professionals were banned from practising their professions. The name of the city of Lodz was changed by the Germans to Litzmannstadt, and they established a ghetto in Baluty, an area which was the city's most impoverished sector, formerly inhabited mostly by criminals and the city's poorest. A total of about 200,000 Jews (this number varied because of deportations and deaths within the ghetto as well as transports from other areas) were confined in the Lodz ghetto,[8] which was completely sealed and closely guarded by Jewish policemen who manned the gates and the perimeter of the ghetto.

The houses were not suitable for human habitation. They were mainly in disrepair and had no heating; the streets were unpaved and turned into slush during the winter months when it snowed. Some ghettos were open, while others were closed or half-closed, but all were guarded. The Jews were completely impoverished and had to live in crowded conditions with several families occupying one room; human waste was thrown into the streets, and contagious diseases spread rapidly under these conditions. The residents had to survive on starvation food rations unless they still had a little money or valuables which they could trade for food smuggled into the ghetto. Many had to beg or steal to survive. Orphans often lived on the streets and had to beg for scraps of food. Small children, who could fit through gaps in the fence or wall surrounding the ghetto, smuggled food into the ghetto. Almost everyone had to work as forced labourers in the ghetto factories and workshops, which functioned for the benefit of the Germans. Those who were not given 'scheins' (work cards) were usually transported to concentration or death camps.

Additional information about some people, places and events

Hans Biebow

The Germans devised a system for administration of the Lodz ghetto to ensure that the many orders and decrees issued by the German authorities were adhered to. Hans Biebow, who had formerly worked as a coffee importer in his home town of Bremen, was appointed to be administrative head for management of the ghetto. Communication between the ghetto inhabitants and the outside world was completely cut off. Food was severely rationed to ensure that the ghetto inhabitants would slowly starve to death. He realised that the ghetto could make a profit for the Germans if it were converted into a slave labour complex. He was a ruthless administrator and exploited the labour force of the ghetto with his ultimate goal being to make the ghetto financially self-sufficient; but he made sure that he personally benefitted from the sale of looted Jewish goods. The ghetto provided him with many opportunities to accumulate considerable wealth. He set up factories and workshops, and he also established warehouses in the town of Pabiance where the Germans stored clothing from the victims killed in the Chelmno extermination camp. The clothing was sent to Germany for use by the German population. Biebow oversaw the transports of people from Lodz ghetto to the Chelmno extermination camp, as well as those who had been brought there from other towns and villages. The last remaining ghettos were destroyed by the Nazis in 1943 and 1944, with the surviving Jews being transported to concentration camps, death camps or labour camps.

After the war, Biebow went into hiding, but he was arrested in Bremen and subsequently stood trial and was convicted of all charges laid against him. He was executed by hanging on 23 June 1947.

ADDENDUM

Chaim Mordechai Rumkowski

During the period that Biebow was in charge of running the Lodz ghetto, a Jewish administrative body called the 'Altestenrat' (Council of Elders) was appointed to aid the Nazis by carrying out their orders and bans concerning the ghetto inhabitants. The occupation authorities appointed Chaim Mordechai Rumkowski to the position of 'Eldest of the Jews', or Head of the Judenrat in the ghetto. At the behest of Biebow, Rumkowski in turn appointed the Council of Elders which supposedly had the role of an advisory body, but the real power lay in Rumkowski's hands. Historians have deemed Rumkowski either a traitor and collaborationist, or a man sincere in his belief that Jews would be safe from transportation if the ghetto could become financially viable. He saw himself as a saviour of the Lodz inhabitants, but he took full advantage of his position of power. The establishment of 120 factories and workshops in which the Jews provided the labour made Lodz a thriving industrial hub. The benefit from the goods manufactured in the ghetto was supposedly for the German war effort. However, the Nazi officers in the ghetto were quick to make use of the factories, and to order whatever they wanted for their personal use. Jewish slave labour did at least receive a slightly better ration of food in order to keep them working for longer. The Jewish Congregation, with Rumkowski at its head, agreed to supply the labour force for the Germans, and it was the Judenrat that recruited the workers. Rumkowski was given considerable independence in running the affairs of the ghetto. He had the authority to create new offices and departments and he also had the authority to arrest people and to be involved in judicial matters concerning the ghetto inhabitants. He was also responsible for providing necessities like heat, housing and other services for the ghetto population. He regarded the ghetto as his own domain and he lived in great luxury. He had his own carriage with a driver, he frequently entertained on a lavish scale, and always provided available women for his cronies. He was known to sexually abuse young girls, one of whom he married.

As soon as the ghetto was established, the Germans demanded that the Jews give up their legal currency and exchange it for ghetto money. Such was Rumkowski's pride that he had the paper notes embellished with a picture of his face. Ghetto postage stamps were also printed with an image of Rumkowski on them. He treated the Jews of the ghetto in a dictatorial manner. Ghetto Jews were being sent to the extermination camp of Chelmno and it was Rumkowski's duty to select the victims to be deported. His most infamous request followed the demand from the Germans that he round up the children and the elderly in the ghetto. Rumkowski delivered a speech to the ghetto community to persuade them to give up their children so that the adults might survive as the workforce. This betrayal of the Jewish community became known as Rumkowski's most evil action. He believed that by doing this the adults would have a greater chance of survival if they continued to work as slave labourers for the Nazi cause.

The Jewish police were organised by Rumkowski at the behest of the Nazis. They numbered about 1200 men in 1943. They wore identifying armbands, caps and badges, but were not given uniforms. Young men were attracted to the police force because they believed that they would be given certain privileges and would avoid deportation. Their duty was to guard the ghetto exits, to maintain order in the ghetto, and to assist with round-ups and deportations of the Jews. Among them were those who hounded the Jews with the same cruelty as the Germans and were corrupt, but there were also those who did what they could to protect the victims and even to aid the underground movement.

In August 1944, Rumkowski and his family were finally transported to Auschwitz, where he was murdered by some of the camp inmates. Lodz was liberated by the Soviet army in January 1945.

Historians are divided in their opinion of Rumkowski, and he remains a controversial figure until the present day.

Amon Goeth

In February 1943 Goeth was appointed Kommandant of the Krakow-Plaszow forced labour camp in the Podgorze area in German-occupied Poland. He soon became known as 'The Butcher of Plaszow' for his sadism and random killings. He was Austrian by birth and had joined a Nazi youth group when he was seventeen. Later he was transferred to the SS, where he was regarded as a model officer. After he was posted to Plaszow, camp conditions for the prisoners became fraught, with collective punishments, torture and death common. Minor transgressions were punishable by hanging or shooting. Goeth devised terrible methods of punishment, frequently using his two dogs to tear victims apart and to feed on them while they were still alive.

He was tried as a war criminal after the war by the Supreme National Tribunal of Krakow and was found guilty of personally ordering the imprisonment, torture and extermination of people. He was sentenced to death and he was hanged on 13 September 1946. He showed no sign of contrition when he was going to be put to death, and even saluted the Führer before dying.

Plaszow labour and concentration camp

The SS in occupied Poland established Plaszow forced labour camp for Jews in 1942. It was later converted to a concentration camp. The camp site included two Jewish cemeteries, which were destroyed when the camp was being built by prisoners. Later the headstones from the cemetery were used as paving stones, or crushed for road construction. An electric fence surrounded the camp area, which contained factories, warehouses and separate accommodation for men and women. At one point the number of people incarcerated in Plaszow was 20,000.[9] The prisoners came mostly from the Krakow ghetto after it was liquidated in March 1943. The guards were mostly Ukrainians, both men and women, who took pleasure in brutalising the prisoners. Many people died of typhus and starvation, as well as from the brutality of camp personnel.

Oskar Schindler, a German industrialist, established an enamelware factory adjacent to Plaszow. There he employed about 900 Jewish workers, whom he tried to protect from being deported to killing centres. He was known to be compassionate to his workers at all times. He used his own fortune to bribe officers, especially Amon Goeth, the camp Kommandant, who was determined to exercise his power over Schindler's workers. Schindler created many schemes and lies about needing all the workers, which he used to deceive the Germans.

In September 1944, Goeth was arrested and charged by the SS with many violations of concentration camp regulations including fraud, theft, starvation of the prisoners and also allowing unauthorised personnel access to documents pertaining to the mass killings. He was replaced by Arnold Buscher, who improved conditions for the camp inhabitants.

ADDENDUM

In 1944, when the Soviet army was approaching Plaszow, the Germans attempted to obliterate all evidence of the mass murders that had taken place there. They exhumed the buried bodies and burned them, later spreading their ashes over the camp area.

The Jedwabne massacre

In the 1930s the Jews of Jedwabne numbered approximately 1500. They accounted for about half the population in the town. The men were mostly tradesmen. The women were housewives and mothers. Some women ran market stalls or little shops. They lived in relative peace with their Polish neighbours until World War II, although the Poles were always willing to apply the old myths and stereotypes to the Jewish population and to suspect that they wielded a lot of power in financial and political matters. These tropes bubbled to the surface whenever there was friction between the Poles and the Jews. It was worse in the cities than in the villages, where Jew and Pole interacted much more. At the start of the war, when Germany invaded Poland, Jedwabne was initially occupied by the Germans, but following the Molotov–Ribbentrop Non-Aggression Pact, agreed upon in August 1939, the Soviets invaded eastern Poland while the Germans occupied western Poland. At first many of the Jews in Jedwabne welcomed the Soviets, assuming that they would be treated more humanely by the Russians than by the Germans. The Poles resented the Jews for their apparent support of communism, and anti-Semitism escalated.

However, the Germans reneged on the pact, and invaded Russia, launching Operation Barbarossa. Fear among the Jedwabne Jews intensified as news of terrible pogroms in other occupied areas of Poland spread. Polish hostility towards the Jews became manifest as young Polish hoodlums looked for Jews to beat with sticks and iron bars. They ordered the hapless victims to burn their holy books, or throw them into the river, and to carry out ridiculous exercises while Polish onlookers laughed at the spectacle. All night on July 10, 1941, Jews were attacked in their houses and taken into the streets where orgies of beatings and torture took place. In his book *Neighbours*, Jan Gross says that 'The massacre of Jedwabne Jews on July 10, 1941, was coordinated by the town's mayor, Marian Karolak.'[10] Karolak played a central role in the pogrom. Gross describes him as 'the evil spirit of this tragedy'.[11] Many uncoordinated and individual attacks on Jews began to take place in different areas of the town and many Jews were killed by beheading, stabbing, clubbing and live burials. Poles began to herd the Jews into the town square. There they were beaten savagely. The Germans, who could have stopped the pogrom, chose not to intervene. Finally, after terribly cruel treatment was meted out to the rabbi and other Jews, they were all pushed into a barn, which was willingly handed over to the mob by the owner. The barn was doused with kerosene and set on fire with all the Jews inside. The victims included men, women and children. Their remains were buried in two mass graves in the ground on which the barn had stood.

After the war, belated trials of twenty-two suspects were held in 1949 and 1950. Only twelve were convicted of treason and one was sentenced to death. Since then, there have been various investigations into the pogrom without any final conclusion about the role played by the Germans and the collaboration of the Poles in Jedwabne.

Posen (Poznań)

Posen is one of the oldest cities in Poland and its history dates back to the tenth century. Jews lived there from about the fourteenth century onwards and were plagued by intermittent anti-Semitic incidents from their arrival. Nevertheless, the Jewish community eventually received equal rights and was considerably influenced in its education and culture by the large German population which had settled in Posen. When the Germans invaded Poland in 1939, many Jews, having learned about the treatment of Jews by the Germans from 1933, fled Posen seeking refuge in other parts of Poland. The Germans marched into the city and immediately closed the schools and took over Jewish businesses.

The first Jewish labour camp was established in the old municipal buildings and commenced operating in the spring of 1941. The Jews were used as forced labourers in public works, construction and transport throughout the city. 'Over 20 labour camps were created in the Posen area. They were: Antoninek, Debiec, Franowo Golecin, Kobylempole, Krzesiny-Piotrowo, and at the end of 1943 there were still some four to five thousand Jewish prisoners there.'[12] Conditions in the camps were appalling and hunger and terror reigned over them.

Fort VII was one of a ring of defensive forts built around Posen in the nineteenth century. It was the first site for a concentration camp in occupied Poland, and later in 1939 the fort was utilised as a Gestapo prison. The first prisoners to be executed there were mentally ill patients and the staff who looked after them. They were exterminated by experiments with gas as a killing medium, and about 400 persons, including psychiatric nurses and doctors, were murdered in Fort VII by the Germans.

Conditions in the camp were especially harsh. Prisoners had no access to washing facilities and slept on the floor on rotting straw.

Prisoners were subjected to starvation and torture. Disease was rife, and spread rapidly.

The Germans decided to liquidate the camp in 1943 in order to use Fort VII as an industrial facility. It was used by Telefunken as a factory for their radios. Meanwhile, prisoners were forced to build a new camp south of Poznań. When the war ended the Poles used the fort as a storage facility.

NOTES

Foreword

1. United States Holocaust Memorial Museum, 'Research an Individual', https://www.ushmm.org/remember/resources-holocaust-survivors-victims/individual-research/services/getting-started, accessed 28/06/2023.
2. Yad Vashem, 'FAQs – Names' Database', https://www.yadvashem.org/archive/hall-of-names/database/faq.html, accessed 28/06/2023.
3. United States Holocaust Memorial Museum, What Was the Holocaust?', https://encyclopedia.ushmm.org/content/en/article/introduction-to-the-holocaust, accessed 28/06/2023.
4. Yad Vashem, 'FAQs – Names' Database', https://www.yadvashem.org/archive/hall-of-names/database/faq.html, accessed 28/06/2023.
5. Kurt Jacob Ball-Kaduri, 'Evidence of Witnesses, Its Value and Limitations', in Shaul Esh, editor, *Yad Vashem Studies, Volume III*, Yad Vashem, Jerusalem, 1959, pp. 79–90.
6. Ibid.

Introduction

1. Suzanne D. Rutland. *Edge of the Diaspora: Two Centuries of Jewish Settlement in Australia*. William Collins, New South Wales, 1997, p. 8.
2. Ibid., p. 8.
3. Ibid., pp. 19–20.
4. Ibid., p. 179.
5. T.W. White, 1938, cited in 'Évian Conference', Wikipedia, https://en.wikipedia.org/wiki/%C3%89vian_Conference.
6. Rutland, p. 179.
7. Paul R. Bartrop. *Australia and the Holocaust 1933–45*. Australian Scholarly Publishing, Melbourne, 1994, pp. 244–45.
8. The Kristallnacht pogrom was organised against the Jews of Germany and Austria on 9 and 10 November 1938. The pogrom was a carefully orchestrated attack on Jews, culminating in rioting mobs of Germans perpetrating violence and destruction on Jews and their property. More than 1000 synagogues were looted and set on fire, and Jewish homes, hospitals, cemeteries and schools were vandalised. At least ninety-seven Jews were killed.

NOTES

9   Displaced Persons camps were known as DP camps and their occupants as DPs; they housed most of the persons displaced by the war before they were repatriated to their country of origin. Most of the Jewish survivors, especially from Eastern Europe, were unable to return home because of local antagonism and prevailing hatred of Jews. For most Jews, all of the Nazi-occupied countries had become a cemetery.

10   The Joint is a non-profit Jewish organisation dedicated to bringing relief to disaster areas. It was established in America in 1914. The abbreviation 'Joint' refers to the American Jewish Joint Distribution Committee, also known as the JDC.

11   Michael R. Marrus. *The Holocaust in History*, Key Porter Books, Ontario, 2000, p. 1.

12   She'erit Hapletah, meaning 'surviving remnant', is a biblical term used by Jewish survivors of the Holocaust in reference to themselves. It is to be found in Ezra 9:14 and Chronicles 4:43 of the Old Testament.

13   YIVO is the acronym for the Yiddish Scientific Institute, which was established in Vilna in 1925. In 1940, they were forced by the war to relocate to New York in America, where their headquarters are at present. Their primary mission is to preserve and perpetuate knowledge of Jewish culture and history.

14   The International Refugee Organization formed an agreement with a number of countries in 1947 concerning the needs of the postwar refugees.

15   Rutland, p. 8.

16   Shoah, the meaning of which is 'destruction', is the Hebrew term for the Holocaust. It was first used in Israel in the 1940s.

17   Ezrahi Sidra De Koven. 'Representing Auschwitz', *History and Memory*, vol. 7, fall 1996, p. 121.

18   Zoe Vania Waxman. *Writing the Holocaust*. Oxford University Press, Oxford, 2006. p. 5.

19   As the main figure to organise the mass deportations of Jews to ghettos and death camps, Nazi leader Adolf Eichmann was put on trial in Israel and was subsequently sentenced to death for his role during the Holocaust.

20   Lawrence L. Langer. *Holocaust Testimonies: The Ruins of Memory*. Yale University Press, New Haven, 1991, p. 1.

21   Ibid., p. 75.

Translator's note on the testimonies

1   The birthplace of Russian-born Shimon Dubnov was the town of Mstsislaw in Belarus. His birth date was 10 September 1860. As an adult, he moved to St Petersburg illegally (Jews were restricted to living in the Pale of Settlement) in 1880, and there he established himself as a historian, writer and activist. After the Jewish population was expelled from St Petersburg, Dubnov moved to Odessa, where he continued to publish studies on Jewish life and history. He was eventually allowed back into St Petersburg, where he became a Professor of Jewish History at Petrograd University. He later emigrated to Kaunus, Lithuania, where his masterpiece, the ten-volume *World History of the Jewish People*, was published

to great acclaim. In 1933 he moved to Riga, Latvia. Riga was subsequently occupied by the Nazis in July 1941 and Dubnov and his family were confined to the Riga ghetto together with the whole Jewish population of Riga. He was murdered by the Germans in December 1941, but shortly before his death he exhorted his fellow Jews to 'write and record' their experiences under the Nazi regime. He is still regarded as one of Judaism's greatest historians.

In German captivity together with Poles

1. Special operations kommando.
2. Gdynia, a port city on the Baltic coast of Poland.
3. Przemysl, a city in southeastern Poland.
4. Macin, a town in the region of Dobrudja in Romania.
5. Galati, a port on the Danube River.
6. German treatment of Jewish captives varied from camp to camp. Jews were always separated from the general POW cohort and would then be placed in slave labour brigades. Sometimes they were transferred to concentration camps.
7. Zakopane is a town in the extreme south of Poland.
8. Lübek is situated in northern Germany in the Shleswig Hostein area. It is situated on the Trabe River and is a major port. It is the largest Baltic harbour of Germany.
9. For information about the Joint, see the Introduction's note 10 on p. 158 in this book.
10. A mezuza is a parchment inscribed with religious texts in Hebrew and attached in a case to the doorpost of a Jewish house as a sign of faith.
11. National Archives of Australia website: http://www.naa.gov.au.
12. *The Hebrew Standard of Australasia*, 24 July 1947, p. 4.
13. *The Daily Telegraph*, 20 July 1947, p. 64.
14. Ibid.

From Lodz to Bergen-Belsen

1. The Jews of Lodz constituted the second largest Jewish community in pre-war Poland. One week after the Germans invaded Poland on 1 September 1939, they occupied Lodz, which they renamed Litzmannstadt. The Germans established the Lodz ghetto in February 1940. Approximately 160,000 Jews were forced to move into the ghetto, where they were confined under the most brutal conditions. In 1941 and 1942 an additional number of Jews from various areas were brought to the Lodz ghetto. In January 1942 the Germans began to transport Jews to the Chelmno killing centre. There, about 70,000 Jews and thousands of Roma were murdered. The deportations came to a halt in May 1944 when the Germans demolished the ghetto. (From the United States Holocaust Memorial Museum. *Holocaust Encyclopedia*, https://encyclopedia.ushmm.org/content/en/article/lodz, last updated 9 August, 2021.) See the Addendum for additional information concerning the Lodz ghetto.

NOTES

2 Marysin was a very poor area, originally inhabited by a large number of underworld characters. The Germans always chose the most deprived areas in which to establish ghettos. Many of the houses there were built of wood.
3 Isaiah Trunk. *Lodz Ghetto: A History*. Translated and edited by R.M. Moses. Indiana University Press, in association with the United States Holocaust Memorial Museum, Bloomington, 2006, p. 245. The so-called white guards comprised transport workers from the Provisioning Department and porters from the Baluty Marketplace. Like the Jewish policemen, these auxiliaries received a security guarantee for their own children and parents.
4 Rumkowski (chairman of the Judenrat in the Lodz ghetto) formed co-operative labour groups of Jews to work for the benefit of the Nazi war effort. The Jews who worked in these co-operatives often received special benefits for their work. The rest of the ghetto population was denied any benefits.
5 This may have been a sarcastic comment or an in joke.
6 The word 'barracks' refers to the living quarters for the prisoners.
7 Kapos were prisoner functionaries chosen by guards and given privileges to supervise forced labour and to carry out administrative tasks. They also had the task of overseeing prisoners in their barracks. They were often very cruel in carrying out their duties.
8 'Gypsy' is a perjorative term used to describe Romani people. Its use in this book is as per the langage of the recorded testimonies.
9 Cut rags that were plaited into mats.
10 Hermann Goering was one of the most powerful men in the Nazi Party, and a collector of property ('Hermann Göring', Wikipedia, https://en.wikipedia.org/wiki/Hermann_G%C3%B6ring, accessed 28/06/2023.).
11 Lane's observation from her discussions with Tobcia.

The Jewish police in Plaszow ghetto

1 This enamel factory, located at 4 Lipowa Street in Krakow, belonged to Oskar Schindler, who saved hundreds of Jewish workers. He was later recognised as a 'Righteous Gentile' by Yad Vashem in recognition of his heroic deeds on behalf of his Jewish workers.
2 Such people were referred to as a 'muselmann', indicating they were close to death.

The destruction of Jedwabne

1 'The Jedwabne pogrom was a World War II massacre committed on 10 July 1941 in the town of Jedwabne in German-occupied Poland. At least 340 Polish Jews, including women and children, were murdered, some 300 of whom were locked inside a barn that was set on fire.' From 'Terms for History'. *Quizlet*, 2023, https://quizlet.com/488280522/terms-for-history-exam-2-flash-cards/.
2 The number of Jewish survivors in Jedwabne has generally been estimated at a much lower figure. However, it is impossible to state exactly how many Jews actually survived the massacre.

NOTES

3   The Jews were trying to get help from Christians but were unsuccessful.
4   The Necropolis Springvale is now called the Springvale Botanical Cemetery.
5   Jan Gross, *Neighbours: The Destruction of the Jewish Community in Jedwabne, Poland*. Princeton University Press, Princeton, 2001.

In the camps around Posen

1   Posen is the German name for the city of Poznań, located on the Warta River in west-central Poland, in the Greater Poland region. Princeton University Press, New Jersey, 2001.

2   Arthur Karl Greiser (1897–1946) was born in the province of Posen when it was part of Imperial Germany. He was a German Nazi politician, SS-Obergruppenführer and Reichsstatthalter (Reich Governor) of the German-occupied territory of Wartheland. Greiser was 'one of the persons primarily responsible for organising the Holocaust in occupied Poland and numerous other crimes against humanity. He was arrested by the Americans in 1945, and was tried, convicted and executed by hanging in Poland in 1946'. From 'Arthur Greiser', Wikipedia, https://en.wikipedia.org/wiki/Arthur_Greiser, last accessed 28/07/2023).

3   Muselmann (pl. Muselmänner, the German version of Musulman, meaning Muslim) was a slang term used among captives of World War II Nazi concentration camps to refer to 'those suffering from a combination of starvation (known also as "hunger disease") and exhaustion, as well as those who were resigned to their impending death'. 'The Muselmann prisoners exhibited severe emaciation and physical weakness, an apathetic listlessness regarding their own fate, and unresponsiveness to their surroundings owing to the barbaric treatment' by the Nazis and prisoner functionaries. (From 'Muselmann'. Wikipedia, https://en.wikipedia.org/wiki/Muselmann citing Primo Levi, 'The Truce', in *If This Is a Man*, Abacus, 1987, p. 94; and citing and Danuta Czech, *Auschwitz: Nazi Death Camp*, Auschwitz-Birkenau State Museum, 1996; and citing Johannes Kepler, official website, University of Linz, Institut für Sozial und Wirtschaftsgeschichte.)

4   Unfortunately the interviewee who provided information about Ester and Shlomo's second son didn't mention the son's name.

Once upon a time there was a shtetl, Bendzin

1   'Until World War II, Będzin [known in English as Bendzin] had a vibrant Jewish community. According to the Russian census of 1897, out of the total population of 21,200, Jews constituted 10,800 (around 51 per cent)'. 'According to the Polish census of 1921 the town had a Jewish community consisting of 17,298 people, or 62.1 per cent of its total population'. 'In September 1939, the German army (Wehrmacht) overran this area, followed by the SS death squads (Einsatzgruppen), who burned the Będzin synagogue and murdered 200 Jewish inhabitants'. 'A Będzin ghetto was created in 1942. Eventually, in the summer of 1943,

NOTES

most of the Jews in Będzin were deported to the nearby German Auschwitz concentration camp. Since Będzin was one of the last Polish communities to be liquidated, there are a relatively large number of survivors from there'. (From 'Będzin'. Wikipedia, https://en.wikipedia.org/wiki/B%C4%99dzin#History citing Joshua D. Zimmerman, *Poles, Jews, and the Politics of Nationality*, Wisconsin, University of Wisconsin Press, 2004, Google Print, p. 16; and citing the archived Jewish Historical Institute community database, 'Jewish Historical Institute Education'; and citing Mary Fulbrook, *Dissonant Lives: Generations and Violence through the German Dictatorships*, Oxford, Oxford University Press, 2011, p. 176.)

2   Yom Kippur is the Day of Atonement, an annual fast day in the Jewish calendar. In 1939, Yom Kippur commenced on Friday evening, 22 September, and concluded after sunset the following day.

3   Marcia Feldman. Introduction' in Devi Tuszynski, *Tuszynski Miniatures*. Committee to Honour the 60th Birthday of Devi Tuszynski, Australia, 1975, p. v. A committee was appointed to select which Tuszynski miniature paintings were to be displayed at the National Library of Australia on his sixtieth birthday.

The destruction of Zolochiv

1   Zolochiv, a small city in the Lviv (Lvov) Oblast of Ukraine, came under German occupation on 2 July 1941 and became part of the General Government. It was wrested from the Russians, who had occupied it in September 1939, but who, from 22 June 1941, were at war with Germany (Operation Barbarossa). On the same day that the Germans occupied the town from the retreating Soviet forces, attacks began on Jews by local Ukrainians and farmers, who flooded into the town to welcome the German army. The day after, graves of political prisoners were found in the town, all of the captives murdered by the Soviets before their retreat, and this served as encouragement for the Ukrainians to initiate their own pogrom against the Jews. The pogrom began on 4 July 1941. Over three days 3000–4000 Jews were murdered. The German soldiers were also active in the murders, but the Ukrainians were eager to carry out their bloodthirsty rampage against the Jews. https://en.wikipedia.org/wiki/Zolochiv.

Addendum: Notes pertaining to the testimonies

1   Noah Klieger. 'Army Was Polish, Soldiers Were Jews'. YnetNews.com, 2006, https://www.ynetnews.com/articles/0,7340,L-3302233,00.html.

2   Ibid.

3   The Molotov–Ribbentrop Non-aggression Pact was signed on 23 August 1939, nine days before Germany invaded Poland, and contained a secret protocol dividing Northern and Eastern Europe into German and Soviet spheres of influence in the event of war.

4   United States Holocaust Memorial Museum. *Holocaust Encyclopedia*, https://encyclopedia.ushmm.org/content/en/article/nazi-camps.

NOTES

5   Philip Friedman. 'The Jewish Ghettos of the Nazi Era'. *Jewish Social Studies*, vol. 16, no. 1, 1954, p. 65.
6   Especially Joseph Goebbels, who was appointed by Hitler as Reichsminister for Propaganda and National Enlightenment. His most virulent propaganda was against the Jews. He was in office from March 1933 to April 1945.
7   Ian Kershaw. *Hitler, the Germans and the Final Solution*. Yale University Press, New Haven, 2009, p. 241.
8   Holocaust and Education Research Team. *The Lodz Ghetto 1940–1944*. 2012, http://www.holocaustresearchproject.org/ghettos/Lodz/lodzghetto.html.
9   United States Holocaust Memorial Museum. *Holocaust Encyclopedia*, https://encyclopedia.ushmm.org/content/en/article/plaszow.
10 Jan T. Gross. *Neighbours: The Destruction of the Jewish Community in Jedwabne, Poland*. Princeton University Press, Princeton, 2001, p. 44.
11 Ibid.
12 Holocaust Education and Archive Research Team, http://www.holocaustresearchproject.org/.

BIBLIOGRAPHY

Primary sources
YIVO Committee of Melbourne. *Seven Eyewitness Testimonies: Pages of Pain and Destruction*. Narrated by Jewish Holocaust survivors, Australia, 1949.

Secondary sources
Abzug, Robert H. *Inside the Vicious Heart*. Oxford University Press, New York, 1987.
Aleksiun, Natalia. *Every Jew Witnessed History. Every Jew Ought to Write It Down. The Central Jewish Historical Commission in Poland, 1944–1947*. Polin, vol. 20, Liverpool University Press, Liverpool, 2007.
Ball-Kaduri, Kurt Jacob. 'Evidence of Witnesses, Its Value and Limitations', in *Yad Vashem Studies, Volume III*, edited by Shaul Esh. Yad Vashem, Jerusalem, 1959.
Bartrop, Paul R. *Australia and the Holocaust 1933–1945*. Australian Scholarly Publishing, Melbourne, 1994.
Bauer, Yehuda and Rotenstreich, Nathan. *The Holocaust as Historical Experience*. Holmes & Meier Publishers, New York, 1981.
Baumel, Judith Tydor. 'The Politics of Spiritual Rehabilitation in the D Camps'. *Simon Wiesental Center Annual*, no. 6, 1989.
Berenbaum, Michael. *Witness to the Holocaust*. Harper Collins Publishers, New York, 1997.
Berkowitz, Michael and Patt, Avinoam J. (Eds). *We Are Here: New Approaches to Jewish Displaced Persons in Postwar Germany*. Wayne State University Press, Detroit, 2010.
Brenner, Michael. *After the Holocaust*. Princeton University Press, Princeton, 1999.
Browning, Christopher. *Nazi Policy, Jewish Workers*. Cambridge University Press, Cambridge, 2000.
Browning, Christopher. *Remembering Survival Inside a Nazi Slave Labour Camp*. W.W. Norton & Company, New York, 2011.
Cesarani, David. *Final Solution: The Fate of the Jews 1933–1949*. Pan Macmillan, London, 2016.
Cohen, Boaz. *Bound to Remember – Bound to Remind: Holocaust Survivors and the Genesis of Holocaust Research*. Secolo, Osnabruck, Germany, 2005.
Dean, Carolyn J. *The Fragility of Empathy after the Holocaust*. Cornell University Press, Ithaca, 2004.
Feldman, Marcia. 'Introduction' in Devi Tuszynski, *Tuszynski Miniatures*. Committee to Honour the 60th Birthday of Devi Tuszynski, Australia, 1975.

Friedman, Philip. 'The Jewish Ghettos of the Nazi Era'. *Jewish Social Studies*, vol. 16, no. 1, 1954.

Grodzinsky, Yosef. 'Historical Commissions in the DP Camps: The Resilience of Jewish Identity', in workshop on 'Birth of a Refugee Nation: Displaced Persons in Post-War Europe, 1945–1951'. Remarque Institute, New York University, New York, 2001.

Gross, Jan T. *Neighbours: The Destruction of the Jewish Community in Jedwabne, Poland*. Princeton University Press, Princeton, 2001.

Gross, Jan T. *Fear: Anti-Semitism in Poland after Auschwitz*. Random House, New York, 2006.

Gross, Jan T. *Golden Harvest*. Oxford University Press, Oxford, 2012.

Hartmann, Geoffrey. *The Longest Shadow: In the Aftermath of the Holocaust*. University of Indiana Press, Bloomington, 1997.

Helm, Sarah. *If This Is a Woman: Inside Ravensbruck, Hitler's Concentration Camp for Women*. Little, Brown Publishers, UK, 2016.

Helm, Sarah. *Ravensbruck: Life and Death in Hitler's Camp for Women*. Little, Brown Publishers, UK, 2016.

Hoffman, Eva. *After Such Knowledge*. Public Affairs, New York, 2004.

Holocaust Education and Archive Research Team website, http://www.holocaustresearchproject.org/.

Holocaust Education and Archive Research Team. 'The Lodz Ghetto 1940–1944'. Holocaust Research Project, 2012, http://www.holocaustresearchproject.org/ghettos/Lodz/lodzghetto.html.

Jokusch, Laura. *Collect and Record! Help to Write the History of the Latest Destruction. Jewish Historical Commissions in Europe, 1943–1953*. New York University, New York, 2007.

Kershaw, Ian. *Hitler, the Germans and the Final Solution*. Yale University Press, New Haven, 2009.

Klein, Kerwin Lee. 'On the Emergence of Memory in Historical Discourse'. *Representations*, no. 69, winter 2000.

Klemperer, Victor. *I Shall Bear Witness*. Weidenfeld & Nicolson, London, 1999.

Klieger, Noah. 'Army Was Polish, Soldiers Were Jews'. YnetNews.com, 2006, https://www.ynetnews.com/articles/0,7340,L-3302233,00.html.

Kochavi, Arieh. 'The Politics of Displaced Persons in Post-War Europe 1945–1950', in *Post-War Europe: Refugees, Exile and Resettlement, 1945–1950*. University of North Carolina Press, Greensborough, 2007.

Kolinsky, Eva. *After the Holocaust: Jewish Survivors in Germany After 1945*. Pimlico, London, 2004.

Konigseder, Angelika and Wetzel, Juliane. 'Displaced Persons, 1945–1950: The Social and Cultural Perspective', in *Post-War Europe: Refugees, Exile and Resettlement 1945–1950*, edited by Dan Stone. Gale Digital Collection, 2007.

La Capra, Dominick. *Representing the Holocaust: History, Theory, Trauma*. Cornell University Press, Ithaca, 1994.

BIBLIOGRAPHY

La Capra, Dominick. *History and Memory: In the Shadow of the Holocaust*. Cornell University Press, New York, 1999.

Langer, Lawrence L. *Holocaust Testimonies: The Ruins of Memory*. Yale University Press, New Haven, 1991.

Mankowitz, Ze'ev. 'The Affirmation of Life in She'erit Hapleita'. *Holocaust and Genocide Studies*, vol. 5, no. 1, 1990.

Marrus, Michael R. *The Holocaust in History*. Key Porter Books, Ontario, 2000.

Rees, Laurence. *The Holocaust: A New History*. Penguin Books, Great Britain, 2017.

Rutland, Suzanne D. *Edge of the Diaspora: Two Centuries of Jewish Settlement in Australia*. William Collins, New South Wales, 1997.

Sidra De Koven, Ezrahi. 'Representing Auschwitz', *History and Memory*, vol. 7, fall 1996.

Trunk, Isaiah. *Lodz Ghetto: A History*. Translated and edited by R.M. Moses. Indiana University Press, in association with the United States Holocaust Memorial Museum, Bloomington, 2006.

United States Holocaust Memorial Museum. *Holocaust Encyclopedia*, https://encyclopedia.ushmm.org/.

United States Holocaust Memorial Museum. 'Nazi Camps', *Holocaust Encyclopedia*, https://encyclopedia.ushmm.org/content/en/article/nazi-camps.

United States Holocaust Memorial Museum. 'Plaszow', *Holocaust Encyclopedia*, https://encyclopedia.ushmm.org/content/en/article/plaszow.

Wajnryb, Ruth. *The Silence: How Tragedy Shapes Talk*. Allen & Unwin, Sydney, 2001.

Waxman, Zoe Vania. *Writing the Holocaust*. Oxford University Press, Oxford, 2006.

Yerushalmi, Yosef Hayim. *Zakhor*. The Samuel and Althea Stroum Lectures in Jewish Studies. University of Washington Press, Seattle, 1982.

Young, James E. *Writing and Rewriting the Holocaust*. Indiana University Press, Bloomington, 1988.

Zeitlin, Froma. 'New Soundings in Holocaust Literature: A Surplus of Memory', in *Catastrophe and Meaning: The Holocaust and the Twentieth Century*. Edited by Moishe Postone and Eric Santner. University of Chicago Press, Chicago, 2003.

ABOUT THE AUTHOR

Freda Hodge is a translator who holds degrees in English, Linguistics and Jewish Studies, and has taught at universities and colleges in South Africa and Australia. Fluent in Yiddish and Hebrew, she worked at the Holocaust Centre in Melbourne, conducting interviews with survivors and families.

Also by Freda Hodge

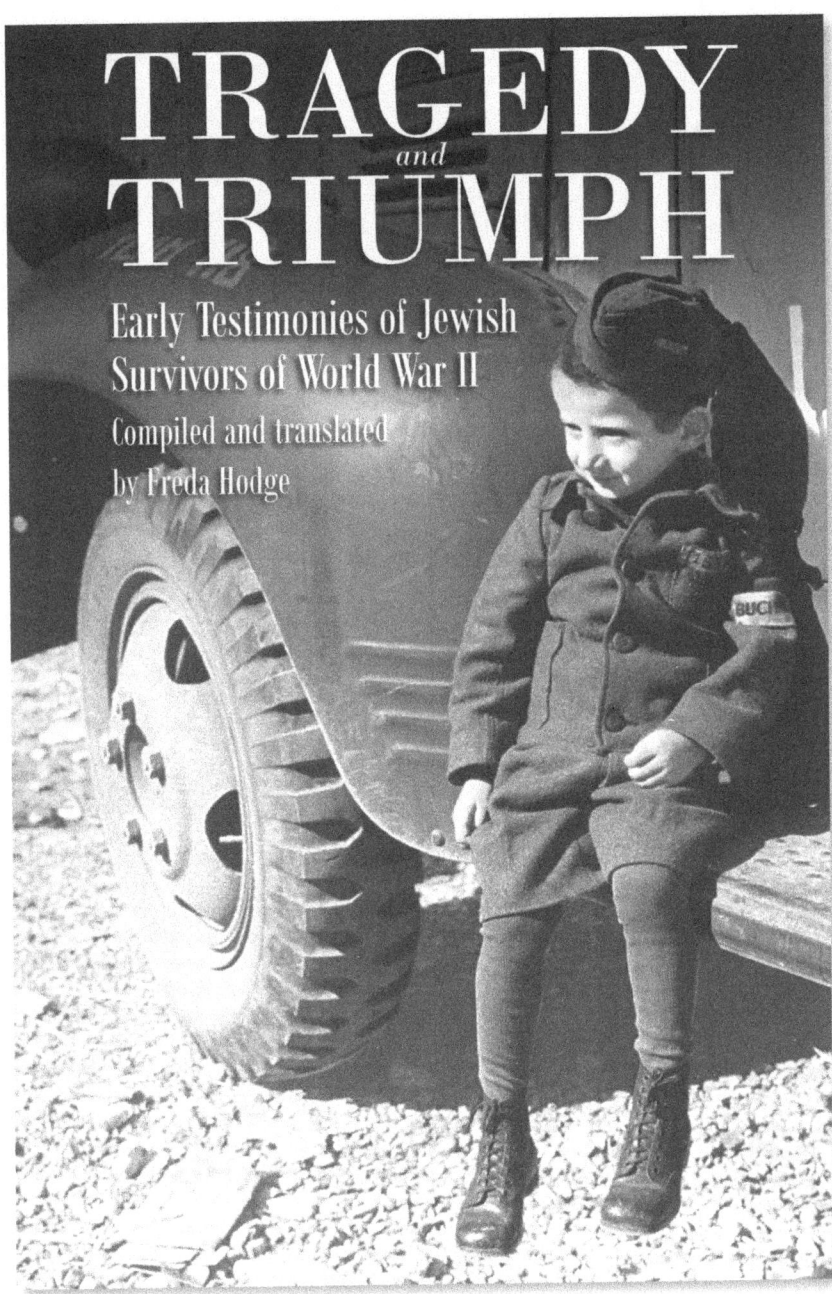